CONTESTED BORDERLANDS

·····································

The Kafia Kingi Enclave
People, politics and history
in the north–south boundary
zone of western Sudan

EDWARD THOMAS

Published in 2010 by the Rift Valley Institute (RVI)
1 St Luke's Mews, London W11 1DF, United Kingdom
PO Box 30710 GPO, 0100 Nairobi, Kenya

RVI EXECUTIVE DIRECTOR: John Ryle
RVI PROGRAMME DIRECTOR: Christopher Kidner
REPORT EDITORS: Emily Walmsley and Aaron Griffiths
REPORT DESIGN: Lindsay Nash
MAPS: Kate Kirkwood
COVER IMAGE: Jonathan Kingdon
PRINTING: Intype Libra Ltd, Elm Grove, Wimbledon, London SW19 4HE
ISBN 978 1 907431 04 3

Contents

LIST OF MAPS

Sources and acknowledgements

This report is based on a survey of scholarly literature and of British-era archives in the UK, and fieldwork in northern and Southern Sudan during 2009 and 2010. Around 200 interviews were conducted, mostly with male interviewees, in different areas of Sudan, including Khartoum, Darfur and Raga county in northern Bahr-el-Ghazal. This allowed representatives of a significant proportion of the groups mentioned in this study to give their views. For security reasons it was not possible to visit the Kafia Kingi enclave itself, or south-west Darfur. Nor was it possible to consult relevant papers in the National Archive in Khartoum

Names of interviewees are not listed. In some cases they requested anonymity, and in others there was not have time during the interview to explain how their names might be used. I am extremely grateful to each of them for their immeasurable contribution to the report, for sharing their time, and for their unexpected support for and fascination with the topic.

I would also like to thank the people who helped me to meet all the interviewees: Paul Annis and Mohaned Kaddam, who helped organize my stay in Sudan; Thiik Giir Thiik and Mohamed Ali, who organized interviews; and al-Fatih Abu al-Qasim who provided transport in Raga.

Several people helped me find documents. Yusuf Takana, Ishaq Aliyu, Ibrahim Abd al-Qadir, Muhammad Aliyu, Suleiman Yahya Mohammad, Robert Futur, Bushera Juma Hussein and Douglas Johnson all gave generous access to their collections of material. In addition to giving me the opportunity to read an extensive collection of papers, Douglas Johnson also kindly provided access to his own notes from archives, which made my time in archives much more efficient. I would like to thank Jane Hogan and staff at Sudan Archive Durham for their assistance during my stay there.

I would also like to credit the work of Ahmad Sikainga: I used his book The Western Bahr al-Ghazal under British Rule (1983) extensively in this study, but I have not cited it much here. It was so popular with people in Raga county that I had to leave my copy there.

Finally, I would like to thank John Ryle of the Rift Valley Institute, who came up with the idea of writing about people living on Sudan's north–south borders in a humane and attentive way, and turned the idea into a project. And Kit Kidner, who makes the projects into realities.

Jonathan Kingdon's cover painting is reproduced by kind permission of the artist. Research for the report and publication of *The Kafia Kingi Enclave* was supported by a generous grant from Humanity United.

Views expressed in this study are the author's alone: they do not represent the view of the Rift Valley Institute or Humanity United or any other organization. The author is solely responsible for any errors.

Note on transliteration

Words transliterated from Arabic texts follow a version of the system adopted by the International Journal of Middle Eastern Studies, without diacritical marks. Words transliterated from oral sources use Roman letters not in that system, like hard g (for the letter qaf), e and o. So the word for an Arabic-speaking cattle-keeper might appear as Baggara or Baqqara depending on whether it is spoken or written. Proper names follow established usage: Mohamed, not Muhammad, and Khartoum, not al-Khartum. Confusingly, Sudanese place names were transliterated on an Egyptian system: Egyptian Arabic has a hard g (for the letter jim) different from the Sudanese hard g (for qaf). This means that Raga and Kafia Kingi, key places in this story, are spelt with a g, but pronounced Raja or Kafia Kinji by Sudanese people.

Most people in Sudan still give road distances in miles, but many use kilometres in other contexts, and that usage is reflected here.

The area under study

This is a study of the western extremity of the border between Darfur and Southern Sudan, with a focus on the Kafia Kingi enclave. Both Western Bahr al-Ghazal (93,900 km2) and South Darfur (127,300 km2) are huge places: respectively, they are roughly the size of South and North Korea, or Portugal and Greece. At 25,000 km2 Kafia Kingi alone is the size of Puerto Rico.

The enclave is sometimes referred to as Hofrat al-Nahas (which means 'copper pit'), after an ancient mining settlement at its northern edge. Its area is roughly contiguous with the Radom Biosphere Reserve, a national park recognised by the United Nations Educational, Cultural and Scientific Organisation (UNESCO) The enclave's territory covers 12,500 km2, roughly the size of Puerto Rico. Formerly part of Bahr al-Ghazal, the enclave is currently under the administration of South Darfur.

This report includes an overview of the history of Kafia Kingi covering the period from the seventeenth century to the present day. During that time place names, administrative boundaries and ethnic groups have all changed, and most administrative terms have changed their range of reference.

Bahr al-Ghazal, which means Gazelle River in Arabic, is a tributary of the White Nile. In the nineteenth century, Darfur was an independent sultanate, and Bahr al-Ghazal was the name for a colonial province that covered the western Nile basin in the south of Turco-Egyptian Sudan. The Kafia Kingi enclave was part of Bahr al-Ghazal province when Sudan gained independence in 1956. In 1960 it was transferred to Darfur, which had become a province of Sudan in 1916. In 1974, Darfur was divided into two provinces, and in 1981 it was made a unified region of two provinces, North Darfur and South Darfur. In 1994, Sudan's nine regions were replaced by 26 states (subsequently reduced to 25). Bahr al-Ghazal region was divided into four states: Lakes, Warrap, Northern Bahr al-Ghazal and Western Bahr al-Ghazal.

Local administrative districts in South Darfur state have become progressively smaller in area since 1974, a development whose political significance is discussed in this report. Since 2009, the enclave has come under Radom locality; before 2009, Radom locality was part of a larger Buram locality (Buram province before 2003); and before 1974, Buram province was part of a larger Nyala province.

The 2005 Comprehensive Peace Agreement requires a return to the 1956 border: if this requirement is implemented, the Kafia Kingi enclave will become part of Raga county in the Southern Sudanese state of Western Bahr al-Ghazal. In 1960, Raga county was called Raga sub-district of the Western district of Bahr al-Ghazal.

The town of Said Bandas appears on many early maps, named after its founder. Most people now call it Boro Medina.

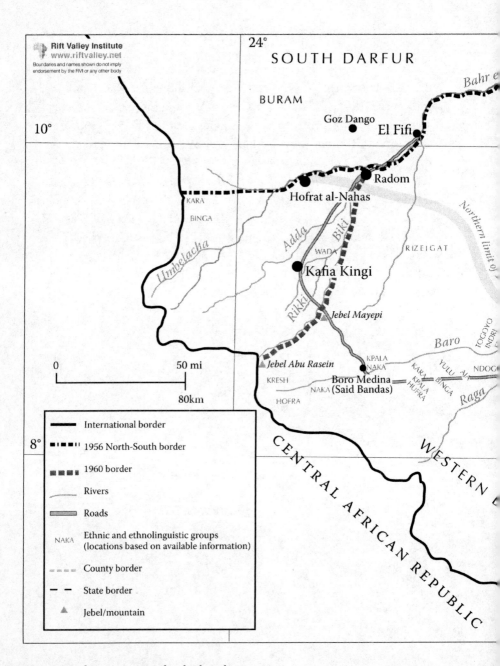

24°

SOUTH DARFUR

BURAM

10°

Goz Dango

El Fifi

Radom

KARA

Hofrat al-Nahas

BINGA

Umbelacha

Adda

Biki

WADA

RIZEIGAT

Northern limit of

Kafia Kingi

Rikka

Jebel Mayepi

Baro

TOGOYO

INDRI

0   50 mi

Jebel Abu Rasein

KPALA
NAKA

KRESH

YULU

NDOG

80km

NAKA

Boro Medina
(Said Bandas)

KARA
KPALA
HUFRA

BINGA

Raga

HOFRA

International border

1956 North-South border

8°

1960 border

Rivers

CENTRAL

WESTERN

Roads

NAKA   Ethnic and ethnolinguistic groups
        (locations based on available information)

County border

AFRICAN

State border

▲   Jebel/mountain

REPUBLIC

Bahr e

Map 2. *Sudan: Western Bahr al-Ghazal*

Sources: Santandrea (1964), Tucker and Bryan (1966).

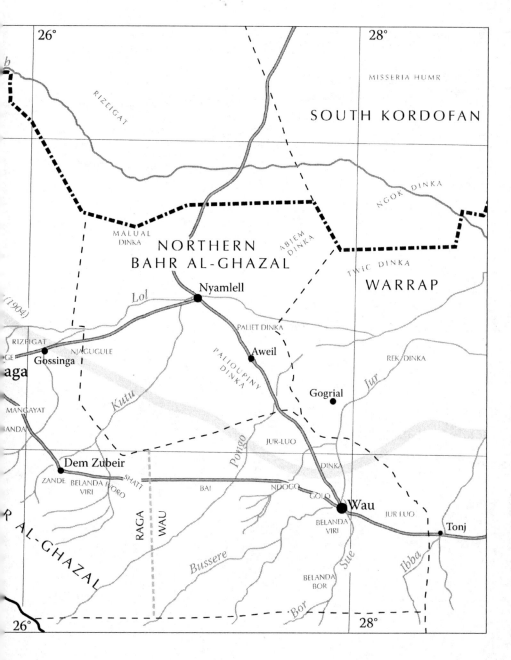

26°   28°

MISSERIA HUMR

RIZEIGAT   SOUTH KORDOFAN

NGOK DINKA

MALUAL
DINKA   NORTHERN
       BAHR AL-GHAZAL   ABIEM DINKA

TWIC DINKA
                              WARRAP

(1904)   Lol   Nyamlell

PALIET DINKA

RIZEIGAT   NJAGUGULE
GE   PALIOUPINY   Aweil   REK DINKA
    Gossinga   DINKA
aga

                                            Jur
                              Gogrial

MANGAYAT   JUR-LUO
ANDA

Kutu   Pongo

                              DINKA

Dem Zubeir   SHATT

ZANDE   BELANDA BORO   BAI   NDOGO
        VIRI   GOLO   Wau

RAGA   BELANDA   JUR LUO   Tonj
WAU   VIRI

R AL-GHAZAL   Bussere   BELANDA   Sue   Ibba
                              BOR

                              Bor

26°   28°

Summary

The Kafia Kingi enclave, sometimes referred to by the name of Hofrat al-Nahas, lies in the savannah belt that runs east–west across Sudan, just south of the Umbelacha River, the westernmost source of the Nile, on the border with the Central African Republic (CAR). It contains forests, copper mines and other mineral wealth. The border area that includes the Kafia Kingi enclave is where Raga, the westernmost county of Western Bahr al-Ghazal, meets Radom locality in South Darfur. It forms part of Dar Fertit, a name derived from a collective term for the peoples of Western Bahr al-Ghazal. Underpopulated, but ethnically complex, peripheral in geographical terms to both north and south Sudan, these remote localities have a special political significance: they are where the north–south civil war, the war in Darfur, and Sudan's multiple peace processes intersect.

The Comprehensive Peace Agreement (CPA) of 2005 between the government of Sudan in Khartoum and the southern-based Sudan People's Liberation Movement (SPLM) envisages an inclusive Sudanese state that invests resources in Sudan's vast, impoverished peripheries. In the words of the agreement, the signatories are required to 'make unity attractive'. The CPA gives the voters of Southern Sudan the opportunity, however, to choose independence instead of unity, in a referendum on self-determination scheduled for January 2011.

The border between north and south Sudan is defined in the CPA as the boundary line of 1956, the year Sudan became independent. At independence Kafia Kingi was part of the south. The area was transferred to northern administration in 1960. Under the terms of the CPA, therefore, it is due to be returned to Southern Sudan, to the administration of Western Bahr al-Ghazal state. The enclave is the largest of the areas along the north–south border due to be transferred to the south.

Here, as in other critical border areas, uncertainty over future administrative arrangements converges with local tensions and wider strategic considerations.

If Southern voters decide on separation in the 2011 referendum Kafia Kingi may find itself on the southern side of a new international border. This possibility has made it the subject of renewed political calculations in Juba and Khartoum. These calculations centre on three features of the enclave. The first is its mineral wealth. Copper has been mined in Hofrat al-Nahas since early times; and there may also be deposits of gold, uranium or petroleum. Second is the enclave's militarily sensitive position in the far west. This is where conflict in Darfur has interacted with conflict in Southern Sudan, most recently in clashes between the Sudan People's Liberation Army (SPLA) and Darfurian pastoralists. For the past two years the Government of Southern Sudan (GoSS) has claimed that the Lord's Resistance Army (LRA), the remnant of a Sudan–Uganda proxy war in the 1990s, has been operating in the area with the knowledge of Khartoum, an accusation denied by representatives of the national government.

The third feature of the enclave is its tradeability. The population of Kafia Kingi is relatively small, somewhere between five and fifteen thousand people, unlikely to be numerous enough to form a constituency that could challenge decisions taken by the parties to the CPA. It is possible that Kafia Kingi could become a bargaining chip in future negotiations between the two parties to the CPA regarding the demarcation of the border between north and south.

This study sets out the available evidence on the history of the north–south border in this part of western Sudan. Before the British colonial period there was no clear delineation of the southern boundary of Darfur, although the Darfur sultanate claimed the copper mines of Hofrat al-Nahas on the southern bank of the Umbelacha River. But in peace deals, presidential decrees and international litigation from the 1970s onwards the Khartoum government has implicitly or explicitly accepted that the enclave is historically part of southern territory.

The report avoids speculation about possible future conflict in Kafia

Kingi. It concentrates instead on the remarkable and little-studied historical experience of the people of this part of western Sudan and the survival strategies they have developed, here and as migrants in other parts of the country. The story of the people of Kafia Kingi and its environs is a reminder that not all the communities of Sudan fit into an easy division between north and south. And their story is repeated, in one form or another, in the experience of many other peripheralized communities in Sudan.

In the early nineteenth century the inhabitants of the area lived outside state structures, practising slash-and-burn swidden agriculture, taking refuge in the inaccessible forests and seasonal marshes of Dar Fertit. The Darfur sultanate recruited labour here, mounting dry-season expeditions that abducted people as slaves or levied them from clients. Slaves were the foundation of the sultanate, both its army and its bureaucracy. Their export was its international trade; their labour realized major state projects, such as irrigation and terraced agriculture; their subordination helped to create the social hierarchy.

The nineteenth-century colonial state transformed this system. It licensed private entrepreneurs to set up permanent settlements in Bahr al-Ghazal. But the establishment of these fortified slave trading centres and the traders' access to supplies of firearms cut off the Darfur sultanate from the source of its wealth and permanently depopulated Bahr al-Ghazal. Slavers' armies eventually overthrew sultanates in Darfur and Central Africa, and the colonial state in Khartoum. The slavers, in turn, were eventually destroyed by twentieth-century European colonialists, whose conquest of Central Africa was many times more devastating than the regimes they succeeded. The study shows how remnants of peoples decimated by these wars often ended up in Raga county: twentieth-century language surveys show that its population was one of the most linguistically diverse in the country.

British administrators under the Anglo-Egyptian Condominium, Sudan's second colonial regime, pursued a conflicting policy: they aimed to develop a cash economy to finance the colonial administration while restricting migration and trade by basing this administration on introverted local chiefdoms. Contact between Darfur and the south was severely circumscribed between 1930 and 1946, with the introduction of a Southern Policy, which was aimed at halting the spread of northern political and cultural influence in the south. Special measures were adopted in the Kafia Kingi enclave, where a highly mixed society used Arabic as a lingua franca, and where some groups had adopted Islam. The British razed the town of Kafia Kingi, and turned the borderlands between Raga and Darfur into a no man's land. For financial reasons, they needed to turn the small and mobile societies of Raga county into a taxable population, and to do so, they forced them to live on a road that linked the major settlements of Western Bahr al-Ghazal: Wau, Raga and Boro Medina. For political reasons, they cut off these small societies from Darfur, where some of them had historical links. This attempt at creating a border to limit Arab Islamic influence from the north ended before independence, but it left a legacy of separate and unequal development and cultural suspicion that contributed to Sudan's subsequent civil wars.

During the first of these civil wars, in the 1960s, many Raga people were involved in the southern insurgency. In Darfur, which was not directly affected by the conflict, joining the government army was a means by which poorer groups participated in the state. But in the second civil war, which began in 1983, the government succeeded in mobilizing people both in Raga and in Darfur into its armies and militias, to combat the new southern insurgency. During the decade of peace between the two wars, changes in southern society had tended to alienate Raga people from other Southerners, a process exacerbated by the actions of the government in Khartoum.

In the 1970s and 1980s the central government was brought close to bankruptcy by the international economic crisis. Instead of investing in its peripheral constituencies, Khartoum pursued a divide-and-rule policy, intensifying local disputes and rivalry over resources. When civil war broke out again, these divisions formed the basis of a counterinsurgency strategy based on the use of ethnically based militias. This further fragmented the societies in Sudan's peripheral regions.

Investment in the economic development of the peripheries was

largely cut off in the 1980s and 1990s. In the 1990s the policy of fragmentation and pursuit of ethnic alliances was accompanied by the promotion
of state versions of Islam. Under the terms of the CPA the government
committed itself to investment in the country's peripheral regions, and
took some steps to reverse the cuts in investment, but, faced with an
insurgency in Darfur, it resorted to the policy of fragmentation and ethnic
alliance-seeking. The CPA period has not provided solutions for Darfur's
divisions and marginalization.

The study examines the narratives of migration and displacement
that emerge from Kafia Kingi and its surrounding areas, linking their
history to the experience of the present day. The wars of the nineteenth-,
twentieth- and twenty-first centuries have dispersed the small language
groups of Raga county across cities and towns in northern and Southern
Sudan. Colonial road building, administrative structures and economic
systems have accelerated this process of urbanization. War and displacement are the means by which the area has been incorporated into the
modern world. The study takes road networks in and between Darfur
and the south as an example of links between modernization, war and
development, examining the historical experiences of the small-scale
societies in their path and the lessons these experiences hold for Sudan
as a whole.

The report concludes with an assessment of the importance of the
western borderlands to Sudan's future. If Sudan remains united after
the referendum, flexible political arrangements will be needed at the
centre of the state. If, as seems more likely, it does not, flexibility will
be needed still more urgently on what will become an international
border. This long border has been presented in many accounts of the
current situation in Sudan as a site of confrontation between distinct
and hostile pastoralist groups, or between victims drawn from one ethnic
group and perpetrators from another. But the reality of the borderlands
is different. This is particularly so in the case of the societies of Western
Bahr al-Ghazal and South Darfur. The historical memories of the people
of these areas are not without bitterness. Yet they acknowledge a history
of cooperation and cultural influence across all divisions of language,

religion and ethnicity. Local memory, and the identities it shapes, is a resource that could form part of the cultural capital of a future Sudan, whether it is one country or two. But equally, these memories could be exploited as a site of conflict between political interests in north or south, seeking to impose simplicity on a complex boundary zone.

1. Introduction

The report divides into three parts. The first five chapters present the historical background. Chapter 2 describes the landscape of the Kafia Kingi enclave, positioned between different ecological and cultural zones. Chapter 3 gives an overview of the different states in the Nile valley, Darfur and Central and Equatorial Africa. One aim of this chapter is to shift the reader's viewpoint from Khartoum, where most Sudanese history is written, to the watershed between the Nile and the Congo, where the enclave lies. Chapter 4 looks at the peoples of the area, with a focus on the hybrid, multi-lingual societies of Raga county, which are known collectively as Fertit. Concluding this first part, Chapter 5 analyses the Southern Policy, from 1930–46, which was the origin of the enclave's no man's land and aimed to create a cultural barrier between north and south.

Chapters 6 and 7, the second part of the report, look at the politics of the border and the economic system of the borderlands. Chapter 6 examines the way that pre-colonial slaving frontiers became colonial borders, and how post-colonial wars and peace deals dealt with the border. Chapter 7 gives an account of the way in which the state extended its reach over society through a road building policy that forced people into villages; and how people fled villages to cities in times of war. Coercive road building illustrates the link between modernization and violence in Sudan's periphery. The chapter also sets out some pointers for the future of roads in Sudan.

The final part of the report, consisting of Chapters 8, 9 and 10, offers a history of Sudan's civil wars from the perspective of the enclave. Chapter 8 looks at the first civil war in the south, and the turn to ethnic politics in Southern Sudan and Darfur. Chapter 9 considers the second civil war in the south, and the SPLA's unsuccessful attempts to use the Kafia

Kingi enclave as a route to take the war into Darfur. Chapter 10 explains how the civil war in Darfur played out in the highly diverse societies on the border. All three chapters set out the social impacts of the wars on everyday life—maintaining the contradictions of the periphery and pushing its people into urban labour markets.

The report concludes by presenting some of the implications of this history for the future: the experience of the enclave and the borderlands around it has lessons for Sudanese people's connections with the state and sense of identity; their trade, livelihoods and labour systems; their relationship with their environment; and the wars that have shaped their histories.

2. Ecological borders and the creation of the Kafia Kingi enclave

In 1956, at Sudan's independence, the border between Bahr al-Ghazal and South Darfur ran along the Nile's westernmost tributary: the seasonal river Umbelacha, which joins the Bahr al-Arab or Kiir River at Radom. In 1960, four years later, the border was moved southwards to a line that follows four other rivers. The official gazette recorded the change:

> From Radom Lat. 9°51, Long. 24°50, which is already inside Darfur Province, the new boundary runs along the right bank of River Adda to Angarbaka village on the junction of River Biki with River Adda. Thence follows the right bank of River Biki to the junction of Rivers Diofo and Sirri and runs along the right bank of River Diofo until its junction with River Rikki. Thence the boundary runs along the right bank of River Rikki to the junction of Khor Uyudidesi with River Rikki East of Jebel Jiowa... Thence crossing River Rikki in a straight line to Jebel Meyepi to J. Tumrogo and thence to J. Abu Rasein on Sudan–Equatorial Africa International Boundary (Republic of Sudan, 1960, p. 473).

The Kafia Kingi enclave, sometimes referred to as Hofrat al-Nahas, sometimes as Dar Fertit and sometimes (in part) as the Radom Biosphere Reserve, is an area of about 12,500 km2 that was transferred from the administration of the Western district of Bahr al-Ghazal province to Buram district in Darfur province. It is the largest of several areas transferred from southern to northern administration after 1956 (no areas were moved from north to south). The Khartoum government that took the decision to shift the boundary from one river to another was following historical precedent: rivers and river basins were used to delimit many of the borders of Southern Sudan. Rivers had been useful markers for Egyptian, British, French and Belgian colonialists, rather than boundaries defined by human settlement, because none of the colonial powers had effective occupation of territory at the time. A 1924 agreement had made the Nile–Congo watershed—a plateau of about 800–1,000 m above sea level—the border between French and British territory in Central Africa. This watershed still defines the border between Southern Sudan and the Central African Republic (CAR), and forms the western boundary of the Kafia Kingi enclave.

The Nile–Congo watershed was a useful reference for foreign cartographers, but for local people it was not such a clear marker. One colonial administrator complained in the early years of the century:

> It is very difficult to make the native understand the
> watershed, and they very much resent being moved from
> some khor [seasonal watercourse], where they have for all
> time been settled because that khor happens to run in a
> certain direction (SAD/542/18/19).

For local people, the valleys of rivers that ran down either side of the watershed were places of settlement and refuge, associated with particular tribes or language groups. Many of these groups spent the nineteenth and twentieth centuries in constant migration and displacement, but when asked by colonial-era ethnographers, they would often give the names of these river valleys as their homes (Reining, 1966; Santandrea, 1981, p. 29).[1]

The rivers of Western Bahr al-Ghazal are mostly seasonal—in the dry season from November to May they turn into streams or pools or dry up altogether. They mostly run north-north-east through the rust-coloured soils of Bahr al-Ghazal's ironstone plateau, a belt of land two or three hundred kilometres wide that lies at the western edge of the Nile basin.

....

[1]   See also tribal lists in SAD/815/7/27–45.

In the savannah areas of Western Bahr al-Ghazal, the acidic soils of the ironstone support glades of mahogany, teak and shea surrounded by grass that dries out in summer. This plateau runs as far south as Equatoria, forming an important ecological border that crosses Southern Sudan. To the east lie the clay soils of the flood plains, seasonally inundated by the rapid run-off of water from the ironstone. The ironstone soils do not retain water, but agricultural yields are more predictable than in the swampy flood plains, where people depend on cattle and fishing instead, along with a little sorghum. This mix of livelihoods—known as agro-pastoralism—is associated with Nilotic groups, such as Dinka and Nuer people (Southern Development Investigation Team, 1955, Vol. I, p. 36, Vol. II, fig. E; Walsh, 1991, p. 45).

The northernmost and westernmost of these rivers running down from the Nile–Congo watershed into the Nile is the Umbelacha—the river that formed the northern border of the Kafia Kingi enclave until 1960, just near the northern limit of the ironstone (SAD/815/7/2). It joins the Bahr al-Arab/Kiir River at Radom, and about 600 km east of Radom the river, by then called the Bahr al-Ghazal, joins the White Nile at Lake No. Just to the north of the Umbelacha the ironstone ends and the stabilized sand dunes or goz that cover most of Darfur begin (Parry and Wickens, 1981, p. 308; Abdalla, 2006, p. 87; Fadul, 2006, p. 36).

The goz of South Darfur supports thinner grassland and smaller, thornier trees than those of Bahr al-Ghazal. The landscape turns a brilliant green in the rainy season even though few seasonal rivers run through it: relatively recent technologies for extracting the shallow ground water have made it into an area of agricultural production. Unlike other soil types in Darfur, it can be cultivated with the hand hoe alone (Hunting Technical Services, 1974; Morton, 2005, pp. 6–9, 51–52).

The twentieth-century 1,000 mm isohyet, the line that marks where rainfall is more than one metre in a year, runs through the Kafia Kingi enclave. But the land here is becoming drier: evidence suggests that the 1,000 mm isohyet is drifting southwards, part of a long history of observed climate change that is putting pressure on the expanding population of Darfur (Morton, 2005, pp. 12–14). The droughts linked to this change in climate are implicated in the migrations and wars in this region, and have also had an effect in Raga county. 'Before 1967 there was water in the *khors* [seasonal rivers] nearly all year round; droughts in Darfur and Chad had an effect in Raga, but because it's rich savannah people didn't notice,' explains al-Fatih Abu al-Qasim of the Raga meteorological station.[2]

Nature reserves in the enclave were first gazetted in the British period, and in 1982 part of the area was listed as a UNESCO Biosphere Reserve (the area covered by the reserve was enlarged in the 1990s). This recognition has not prevented a dramatic decline in wildlife: a 1977 study recorded 24 mammalian species, but a 2003 study found only 11—elephants and antelopes were among those that had disappeared. The enclave's remoteness, and the wars and drought-induced migration since 1977 have pushed people towards hunting as a livelihoods strategy (Hassan et al., 2005, pp. 19–20).

The region's insect population also has implications for human life and livelihoods. The prevalence of tsetse fly in Western Bahr al-Ghazal makes the area unsuitable for cattle. The northern limit of tsetse fly, which can carry human and bovine trypanosomiases, runs through the area, varying with forest cover. As a result, in Western Bahr al-Ghazal few people keep cattle, in contrast to Northern Bahr al-Ghazal—a tsetse-free area to the east—where some of the biggest herds in Sudan are found. Jur river blindness—onchocerciasis—caused by a parasite carried by the black fly, is also endemic in the area: Raga county has one of the highest rates of blindness in the world (Center for Disease Control, 1995).

Insect-borne diseases and the creation of a reserve in the area have both casused population displacement in recent decades. Sheregna village in the Kafia Kingi enclave was evacuated in the 1970s because

....

[2]   Interview with al-Fatih Abu al-Qasim, head of Raga town meteorological station, 17 March 2010.

of Jur river blindness.[3] People living on the Umbelacha River west of Deim Bishara were forcibly moved when the reserve was extended in the 1990s.[4] This displacement is part of a much wider story of migration discussed throughout this report.

The mineral wealth of the region has also shaped the history of its local cultures. Several groups in the area have a history of iron-working that lasted into the twentieth century (Comyn, 1911, p. 262). The region's ubiquitous small rocks of iron ore are the simplest offering in traditional religious rites, and iron hoes form part of bridewealth payments and are incorporated into marriage rituals (Santandrea, 1980, p. 839). The name of a principal settlement in the Kafia Kingi enclave, Hofrat el-Nahas, means 'copper mine' in Arabic. The Ngbongbo people, who are part of a wider group called Kresh that lived in the area in the nineteenth and twentieth centuries, are usually called 'Kresh Hofrat el-Nahas' and contributed to the labour force for the mines.

The mines produced copper until the 1920s, and in pre-colonial days exported it as far as Nigeria (O'Fahey, 1980, p. 135). The copper excited the imaginations of the colonial powers who competed for control over Southern Sudan during the chaotic days of the 1880s and 1890s, when Mahdist, Belgian and French armies marched through the enclave. Anglo-Belgian companies importuned British officials for mining concessions, and Belgian flags flying on the low hills on the east of the Nile–Congo divide caused a brief crisis with the French government before the British conquest (NA/FO/10/776; Santandrea, 1955, p. 188). Surveys at the end of the colonial era found that copper exploitation was not economical. After independence, the Geological Survey Department estimated that the ore deposits could yield 283,400 tons of copper; a Japanese survey in

....

[3]   Interviews with al-Fatih Abu al-Qasim, head of Raga town meteorological station, 17 March 2010; and with Miskin Musa Abd al Mukarram, executive director, Timsah, Raga county, 20 March 2010; see also Santandrea (1964, p. 324).

[4]   From extracts of a report in Arabic on the drugs trade in Radom Biosphere Reserve, which appears to have been commissioned by the South Darfur state ministry of agriculture and livestock in the late 1990s. Provided to the author by an NGO official who is also a member of the NCP in Radom.

1964–65 came up with more modest estimates; and a UNDP survey in 1973 concluded that the fact that several companies had studied it without placing it in production was an indication of its marginal economic potential (UNDP, 1973, p. 101).

Nonetheless, the multinational mining company Billiton conducted surveys in the area from the 1970s until 1999 (Billiton PLC, 1999, p. 44). One miner who worked in Kafia Kingi in the early 1980s commented:

> I worked for two years in the mines, panning. In Sharikat
> Zayn, for gold. There was gold. But that's stopped now with
> the problems. It has silver, it has copper and uranium. But
> there was no uranium mine. It was copper and gold only.
> Billiton came—16 *baburs* [engines or heavy machines] were
> working—for copper and silver and gold. Now they have a
> babur there working still.[5]

Publicly available documents setting out the evidence for the existence of silver, oil, uranium or petroleum are hard to find. Small amounts of gold were discovered in rivers west of Raga during the colonial period, and other sources refer to uranium deposits (SAD/815/7/5). The enclave lies to the south of Block 6, Sudan's westernmost oil concession and some interviewees believed that there may be oil in the area too.

Like most of the north–south border, the Kafia Kingi enclave is rich in resources and delicately positioned. But unlike other areas of the border, it is almost empty of people, partly due to an attempt by the colonial administration to create a no man's land between northern and Southern Sudan, which is discussed in Chapter 5. Population estimates in the 1990s varied between 5,000 and 15,000 people (Hassan et al., 2005, p. 13).[6] The enclave's combination of emptiness and wealth are at the centre of the calculations of elites in Juba and Khartoum, who are required to agree and demarcate the border in fulfilment of the CPA. But this mineral wealth

....

[5]   Interview with retired miner, name and location withheld, April 2010.

[6]   The 5,000 figure is extrapolated from extracts of the same report in Arabic on the drugs trade in Radom Biosphere Reserve, see footnote 4.

lies in a zone of multiple overlapping ecologies, which have helped to shape diverse local cultures, identities and notions of ethnicity. The no man's land was an attempt to get rid of these cultural crossovers, to make a lasting barrier between the cultures of Darfur and Bahr al-Ghazal. The barrier only lasted 16 years, but the memory of a border that divided cultures and languages still has significance today, as Sudan prepares for a referendum on the unity of a multicultural nation.

3. Borders between states and statelessness: Darfur and Bahr al-Ghazal in the eighteenth and nineteenth centuries

For most of the past two hundred years, the principal state projects in Bahr al-Ghazal have been to draw the region into international economic and political systems through war, displacement and ferocious commerce. In the nineteenth century, different states carried out these projects but many written histories focus on the relationship between Bahr al-Ghazal and the Fur (or Keira) sultanate that ruled Darfur from the seventeenth to the twentieth century. The sultanate's slave raiding in Bahr al-Ghazal was vital to its ability to engage in international trade, but its raids probably did not reach very deep into the region (O'Fahey, 1980, p. 137). Further south, in present day Equatoria, Democratic Republic of the Congo (DRC) and CAR, Zande states were established in the eighteenth and nineteenth centuries, also using slavery and slavery-like institutions to incorporate local populations. It was not until the mid-nineteenth century that a regime permanently occupied Bahr al-Ghazal: the Turco-Egyptian colonial state based in Khartoum. The Turkiya (as this state is known in Sudan) franchised its occupation to private slave-raiding entrepreneurs. These entrepreneurs made Bahr al-Ghazal the centre of a new system of raiding and capture that transformed Darfur and Central Africa.

Alongside these states were groups who lived without state authorities governing them, or at the fringes of the state. The relationship between states and these stateless people was based around the state's need for labour, for a taxable population. The state recruited labour in ungoverned areas, by abductions or by levying slaves from clients. Slaves had many uses for the state: they were exported, forming the basis of international trade; their labour was used in major projects such as the terracing of

Jebel Marra, the massif at the centre of Darfur; and they performed difficult or undignified tasks that eased the life of the better-off, helping to
sustain a social hierarchy that could be used to explain the state's central
coercive power. The presence of ungoverned areas at the fringes of the
state presented subjects with the possibility of escaping its coercive and
hierarchical regime by seeking a subsistence life of swiddening (mobile
slash-and-burn agriculture) in the forests to the south of the Umbelecha
and Bahr al-Arab/Kiir rivers. This free, subsistence alternative was not
without risks, however, as the state still tried to capture and enslave the
escapees. In the time of the Darfur sultanate, people who evaded the
state in this way were called Fertit. Similar groups existed in Equatoria
and in present-day CAR (O'Fahey, 1982).

The border between state power and statelessness, between slavery
and subsistence, is explored in this chapter and the next. For a long time
it was the most significant social boundary overlaying the many ecological borders described in the previous chapter. Its existence eventually
provided a justification for the colonial decision to create a no man's land
along the border, a policy partly aimed at suppressing the slave trade.

Fugitive swiddening was not the only way to evade the state: pastoralism offered another alternative. In the period under study, as today,
mobile societies of Nilotic cattle-keepers lived in the hard-of-access
clay plains of eastern Bahr al-Ghazal, and other groups of cattle-keepers
occupied the more accessible southern savannah lands of Darfur. Darfurian cattle-keepers today are nearly all Arabic speakers, mostly with
distinctive origin stories that link them to the political and religious
celebrities of the first Muslim empires in the Middle East, or Tunisia and
Andalusia (Aliyu, 2008, p. 1). Arabic-speaking cattle-keepers eventually
spread out across a belt between the tenth and thirteenth parallels in
between present day Nigeria, Lake Chad and the White Nile. In Darfur,
they are based on the north of the Bahr al-Arab/Kiir River, in an area
where the state had less authority as it was cut off in the wet season
(Mahmud, 2006, pp. 43–48; Aliyu, 2008, p. 1). In Sudan, these herders
are called Baqqara or Baggara (Arabic for cattle-keeper). In other Sahelian
countries, they are sometimes called Arabs.

In the twentieth century, the lorry and helicopter dramatically extended the state's reach, transforming the way that people in this area participated in or evaded its rule. In order to understand the extent of these changes, which have been key to the wars and migrations of the twentieth and twenty-first centuries, it is useful to look back at the state systems of the nineteenth century and before. In Bahr al-Ghazal and Darfur, these were: the Fur sultanate, Zande states, the Turco-Egyptian state (Sudan's first colonial state), and the Mahdist state. The following summaries of each system also make brief reference to states in present-day CAR, whose history was once closely linked to that of Bahr al-Ghazal.

The Fur sultanate (seventeenth century to 1916)

The Fur people are a language group whose origin stories lie in the fertile uplands of Jebel Marra, the massif at the centre of Darfur. They expanded southwards, probably by incorporating other groups, a process that was accelerated by Darfur's independent Fur (or Keira) sultanate. The Fur sultanate began in the seventeenth century: a sultan with an Arab father and a Fur mother drove out an old sultan and established Islam. The story of this Arab patriarch transforming an African society by exploiting its matrilineal systems is still used to explain historical development in Sudan today.

At the time, states across the Sahel, from the northern Nile valley to Nigeria, were adopting a similar Muslim political repertoire, which shaped their relationship with partially-incorporated client groups to the south: Baggara groups, fugitive societies over the border, and stateless societies in the interior. Together, these states and the groups living on their southern margins were drawn into the Middle Eastern economy, and slavery played a central role. Long-distance trade in slaves and forest goods brought firearms and luxuries from the Arab cities of the Middle East. Baggara groups helped to organize this trade, participating in state-sponsored expeditions to abduct slaves or levy them from terrorized client groups. They also used the southern hinterland to pasture their animals or to evade the state's power. Some small-scale societies south of the Baggara belt may have lived there before seventeenth-century states were formed. Many people in Bahr al-Ghazal and the north-eastern Congo basin are descendents of the fugitives, maroons, dissidents or members of pre-Keira regimes in Darfur who were pushed southwards by politics or taxes (O'Fahey, 1980, pp. 29–30, 73).

Zande states (mid-eighteenth century to 1900)

A network of Zande states, nearly all of them led by a ruling elite known as the Avongura, covered territories in present-day CAR and DRC. They were part of the Great Lakes region, rather than the Sahel, and state practices differed significantly from those of the sultanates to the north. In the Nile basin, members of the Avongura ruling house colonized areas of Equatoria and Bahr al-Ghazal with the Ambomu Azande, people of the Mbomou River in present-day CAR. They migrated eastwards in the eighteenth century, conquering vast territories on either side of the Nile–Congo divide. The amalgam of the migrating and conquered groups, under centrally organized military and judicial systems, created the Zande people of today. Ambomu settlers and elite appointees would live with assimilated groups, drawing them into new conquests and enslavements. This assimilation was only partial: in the mid-twentieth century, the people calling themselves Zande spoke languages from all the different major African language families (Evans-Pritchard, 1963, pp. 134–54; 1971, pp. 268–71).

In Bahr al-Ghazal, the Zande state, like the Fur sultanate, incorporated the stateless people of the interior into their new order through slavery. In the eighteenth and nineteenth centuries, as the region became more deeply engaged in Middle Eastern markets and more exposed to international religious learning, some states began to use Islamic explanations and justifications for the expanding slave trade: peoples of the interior were seen as 'enslaveable' because they were not Muslims. Some contemporary Muslim observers, such as the Tunisian writer Muhammad bin Umar al-Tunisi (el-Tounsy, in a better-known French rendering) rejected this use of the sources of Islam. Al-Tunisi lived in the sultanates of Darfur and Wadai in the early nineteenth century, and noted that enslavement by abduction or levy, and without the offer of conversion or an agreement to live as peaceful tributaries of the Islamic state, contravened Islamic law (Al-Tunisi, cited in Clarence-Smith, 2008, p. 12). But the notion of the 'enslaveability' of non-Muslims gave slavery an enduring set of cultural meanings, which still resonate today in discussions about border relationships.

The first colonial state: the Turkiya (1821–85)

In 1821 an army from Ottoman Egypt conquered Sudan. Its principal aims were to acquire gold and slaves, needed as conscripts for the Egyptian army, which was being modernized in order to serve the expansionist aims of the Egyptian ruler, Muhammad Ali. The Turkiya, as the regime is known in Sudan, transformed slavery and the military and trading systems of the state. In the 1850s, the new regime licensed Sudanese, Middle Eastern and European traders to take over a government monopoly on ivory that it had established in the south, but by 1860 most traders had switched to the more lucrative slave trade, with Bahr al-Ghazal as its centre (Gray, 1961, pp. 21, 37; Gessi, 1892, p. 1). Darfurian raiders had previously come in dry-season expeditions, but the Turkiya traders established permanent forts or *zaribas*, some with thousands of armed personnel. Slave traders sought the support of Islamic law for their activities—even Christian slave traders flew banners with Quranic exhortations to *jihad* or religiously-sanctioned warfare. (Jihad is a key element of the justification of slavery in Islamic law, although nearly all authorities today reject the self-serving legal reasoning of the slavers) (Mire, 1986, p. 115).

The private armies of Turkiya entrepreneurs were made up of local slave conscripts along with deserters from the Egyptian Army and farmers from the northern Nile valley, dispossessed by the heavy taxation of the colonial state. Military slaves learned about new weapons and military strategies while fighting alongside northern captors: their new skills soon changed Sudan for good.

Economic and military transformations in Bahr al-Ghazal weakened the Fur sultanate in the second half of the nineteenth century. It was forced to improvise with new administrative and tribal orders on its troubled southern border, which played out over several decades of war between sultans and Baggara groups (O'Fahey, 1980, pp. 12, 42, 98ff). From the 1860s Bahr al-Ghazal's slavery system came under pressure from European (and some Egyptian) abolitionists, alongside European powers seeking to legitimize their penetration of Africa (Baer, 1969, p. 188). Egypt began suppressing the transportation of captives on the White Nile—until then, the main trade route north. Instead, Bahr al-Ghazal slavers sought to negotiate alternative routes to Mediterranean markets with Baggara leaderships in Darfur, themselves under pressure from the Fur sultanate, and in search of pastures and a place in the Bahr al-Ghazal slavery system. The breakdown of one agreement on trade routes was a motivation for the 1874 invasion of Darfur led by Zubeir Pasha, one of the most powerful and ambitious slavers, after whom the settlement of Deim Zubeir is named (Theobald, 1965, p. 21). Zubeir's army, from the Nile valley and Bahr al-Ghazal, defeated Baggara and Fur armies and incorporated Darfur into Turkiya Sudan (Cordell, 1985, p. 18). Zubeir's conquest of Darfur gave him enormous powers, and Turkiya authorities soon decided that he posed too great a threat. The government in Cairo ordered him not to interfere in the affairs of the state, and in 1875, when he went to Cairo to present his case to the authorities, he was arrested (Jackson, 1913, pp. 77–78). His son and followers remained in Sudan, where they were defeated by Romolo Gessi, the Turkiya governor of Bahr al-Ghazal, in 1879. Gessi and his successor held Bahr al-Ghazal for only five years, before the next convulsion of conflict swept the Turkiya away.

The Mahdiya (1882–85)

The Sudanese Mahdi, Muhammad Ahmad, the religious and political leader who led resistance to Turco-Egyptian rule in Sudan in the late nineteenth century, announced his mission in 1882. His revolution, and the regime it created, was called the Mahdiya. The Mahdi means 'the

FIGURE 1.
OFFICIAL POPULATION FIGURES FOR RAGA COUNTY

Year	Population	Source
2008	54,230	Census
1999	64,650	Province HQ estimate
1983	48,289	Census
1956	35,526	Census

Sources: Republic of Sudan (1957); Democratic Republic of the Sudan (1983); Sudan Transition and Recovery Database (2003, p. 3); Southern Sudan Centre for Census, Statistics and Evaluation (2009, p. 5).

FIGURE 2.
POPULATION OF WESTERN BAHR AL-GHAZAL AND NEIGHBOURING STATES IN 2008 CENSUS

State	Ecology	Population
Western Bahr al-Ghazal	Ironstone plateau	333,431
Lakes	Flood plain	695,730
Northern Bahr al-Ghazal	Flood plain	720,898
Warrap	Flood plain	972,928
South Darfur	Mostly goz near border	4,093,594

Sources: Census returns for Darfur in Presidency of the Republic (2009, p. 7); for Southern Sudan in Southern Sudan Centre for Census, Statistics and Evaluation (2009, pp. 2, 5).

causing enormous human losses and sending large populations into captivity or into refuge in Western Bahr al-Ghazal (Cordell, 1985, p. 29). Mahdist, French and Belgian armies crossed Bahr al-Ghazal without establishing permanent control, while Zande armies from the south raided for slaves. The peoples of Darfur's southern borderlands were joined by people from the Central African interior: remnants of groups shattered by a new kind of war, surviving through escape, bush-living, clienthood and subordination.

State penetration and changing demographics in nineteenth century Bahr al-Ghazal and Central Africa

In many respects, Western Bahr al-Ghazal has not fully recovered from its long, conflict-ridden nineteenth century. The slave raids and colonial conquests of that period created huge population displacements that have left the region relatively unpopulated still today. Raga county, the current name for the westernmost district of Western Bahr al-Ghazal state, is the largest and least populous county in Southern Sudan, with only 54,320 people in the 2008 census. The 2008 census was controversial, because it allegedly under-counted constituencies likely to oppose the NCP in Darfur and Southern Sudan (Thomas, 2010, p. 13). But previous censuses (which are probably no more precise than that of 2008) show that Raga has been under-populated since the mid-twentieth century. Colonial population estimates were based on taxpayer numbers, and taxpayers were organized by tribe. Taxpayer numbers in most Raga tribes declined between 1927 and 1952 (Santandrea, 1964, pp. 321, 329).

The whole of Western Bahr al-Ghazal's ironstone plateau—the Fertit homeland—appears almost as a blank on the population map. But the surrounding areas—the flood plains to the east and the goz areas to the north—are much more populous.

Part of the reason for the under-population of Fertit areas relative to other areas lies in soil and hydrology—the ironstone plateau does not retain water and has poor aquifers, unlike the goz and the flood plain. But this fact alone does not account for such a small population in such guided one', a figure who is mentioned in some collections of the teachings of the Prophet Muhammad, and who is associated with the end times. These teachings inspired controversies and revolts in different eras, sects and regions of the Islamic world. In Sudan, Muhammad Ahmad al-Mahdi was able to mobilize the aspirations of disaffected slave soldiers, over-taxed peasants and pastoralists, and people turning to religion after 60 years of violent economic and social change. With this following, he led an army (with many Baggara and Bahr al-Ghazal troops) that took Khartoum in 1885. He died within six months of its capture. His successor, the Khalifa Abdullahi al-Tayshi, was from the Taysha group of Baggara people from the Darfur–Bahr al-Ghazal border. Central to the revolution and to the regime's control of the state were the newly militarized border groups from the west—both those defined by ethnicity, such as the Baggara, and those defined by slavery, such as the bazingers of the slave armies. The Khalifa recruited armies from formerly stateless groups of Bahr al-Ghazal, and forcibly moved whole populations of Baggara people to Omdurman, where the most expensive neighbourhoods still bear the names of the security forces from that distant era.

Central Africa and the arrival of European colonial power (1878–1900)

The end of the Turkiya linked Bahr al-Ghazal's long conflict to new crises in the Congo basin. After Gessi's victory in 1878, one of Zubeir's lieutenants, Rabih Fadlallah, escaped across the Nile—Congo watershed, where the end of the Bahr al-Ghazal slaving system and the arrival of French colonialists from the west briefly offered opportunities for adventurers and subordinate states. Rabih overran Dar al-Kuti and Dar Runga, two southern clients of the Wadai sultanate (located in present-day CAR), and installed Muhammad al-Sanusi as ruler of Dar al-Kuti in 1890. Together they used captured French guns to establish the firearms-and-zariba system of Bahr al-Ghazal slave raiding in an area where slave capture had previously followed the expedition system of the Wadai and Darfur sultanates. This shift set off several decades of war and displacement, a huge place. The demographic pattern reflects histories of violence, and the comparable population data for neighbouring prefectures in present-day CAR, where many Raga groups have their origin, bears out this past. Haut Mbomou, which covers an area of 55,530 km2, had 33,019 people in 1975 but only 27,382 in 1985; Haute Kotto and Vakaga, the other two bordering prefectures caught up in the same nineteenth and twentieth century wars, have comparable population sizes and densities (République centrafricaine, 1978, p. 23; République centrafricaine, 1989, p. 96).

The populations of Raga and Vakaga were incorporated into the international economic system during the period covered in this chapter. Incorporation came at great human cost. Romolo Gessi, the penultimate Turkiya governor of Bahr al-Ghazal, estimated that in 14 years of slaving, 400,000 people were taken from Southern Sudan (he called it 'the Soudan of the Nile') and that 'thousands and thousands were massacred in the defence of their families' (Gessi, 1892, p. 2). Zubeir's lieutenant Rabih Fadlallah transferred that kind of warfare to Dar al-Kuti in present-day CAR, decimating groups such as the Yulu, Kresh, Sara and Banda—many of whom lived in places like Vakaga and Haute Kotto, and who fled to Raga, where many live today.

France's violent pacification of the area, in the early years of the twentieth century, brought many more deaths. Ayoub Balamoan, a historical demographer, estimates that during the period from 1906 to 1925 three to four million people were forced to move between French and Belgian Equatorial Africa, and that about half of them died on the way. French pacification lasted till 1923, by which time it had killed about half the total population (Balamoun, 1981, pp. 208–09). The slavery, forced labour and routine atrocity of those days were publicized by the French Nobel prize-winning novelist André Gide and others (Gide, 1927; Kalck, 2005, p. xxviii).

Banda tribes live on both sides of the Nile–Congo watershed and some fled from French pacification to Raga (Santandrea, 1964, pp. 247–8). Today, non-Banda people sometimes jokingly remind them of their alleged history of cannibalism.[7] Documentary evidence suggests that cannibalism was forced on the local population by the extreme violence of the colonial system, whose compulsory rubber cropping and forced porterage undermined people's ability to survive. A French priest explained the social effects of French forced labour in the early twentieth century:

> The sick and little children who had been abandoned in
> the villages died of hunger there. Several times I visited a
> region where those who were ill did their best to feed them;
> and there I saw open graves from which the corpses had
> been removed to serve as food... As a consequence of this
> lamentable state of affairs, numerous villages survived simply
> as ruins; plantations ceased to exist, and the population
> was reduced to the direst misery and despair. Never had the
> people lived through such horrors, even during the worst
> periods of the Arab invasion (R.P. Daigre, quoted in Suret-
> Canale, 1971, p. 33).

British and Belgian colonialists also used forced labour and compulsory cotton cropping to control and extract wealth from the populations they administered (though British administrators did not use the term 'forced labour' to describe their systems of tax labour and of prison labour by tax defaulters) (Reining, 1966, p. 87; Suret-Canale, 1971, p. 31). Raga county people would sometimes escape from one jurisdiction to another and then go back again, possibly in response to the introduction of coercive policies. For example, Yulu people crossed the border under pressure from the Dar al-Kuti system; returned to French-controlled areas when the British tried forcibly to move them from Deim Zubeir in 1912; and then came back to Raga county around 1922 (SAD/815/7/45; Santandrea, 1964, p. 232).

The recurrence of crisis and neglect is a feature of histories of the

....

[7]   Interview with Raga people, 7 March 2010.

periphery. In the late nineteenth century the Bahr al-Ghazal–Darfur border, now the emptiest section of the 2,100 km border between north and south Sudan, was where the periphery violently redefined the centre of Sudan. The system that the Turkiya established there eventually destroyed the independent sultanate of Darfur and provided the military basis for the Mahdist revolution.

But these transformations exacted enormous human costs. Demographic evidence suggests that Fertit areas paid a higher price than other groups who underwent the same history—their areas are emptier. Part of the reason for this emptiness lies in nineteenth policies of coerced labour and displacement caused by war. In the twentieth century, these policies were continued, pushing people from Raga county towards cities, towns and markets in Bahr al-Ghazal and across Sudan. The next chapter looks more closely at who exactly these Fertit people were.

4. Being Fertit: people and societies in Western Bahr al-Ghazal and the Kafia Kingi enclave

The people of Dar Fartit are slaves and [yet] go free.[8]

In pre-colonial Darfur, 'Fertit' was a word for people with low status but enviable possibilities of freedom from state control and of self-sufficiency. The wars of the nineteenth century changed this meaning, with the term coming to refer to a more diverse population of people who had fled from Darfur and wars in Central Africa to Bahr al-Ghazal. This chapter tries to explain that diversity by setting out different approaches to defining what it means to be Fertit. Languages, histories of slavery, political affiliations, religious affiliations and cultural practices are all categories illustrating differences between Fertit groups. Examining those categories serves to show the impossibility of reducing the diverse peoples of Kafia Kingi to a ready schema: the area under study is one of Sudan's 'shatter zones', a place broken by the violence of the nineteenth century and left with the remnants of different populations.[9]

The final paragraphs of this chapter briefly describe the groups of people who live to the north of the Kafia Kingi enclave, many of whom are seasonal visitors to the area.

....

[8] Fur song quoted in O'Fahey (1980, p. 73).

[9] The term comes from Professor Wendy James. On other 'shatter zones' in Sudan, see Ewald (1990); for an account of comparable historical processes in the very different setting of South-East Asia, see Scott (2009).

Languages

Although Western Bahr al-Ghazal's population is small, it is one of Sudan's most culturally diverse regions. A look at 24 selected languages spoken in the state (see Figure 3) shows something of that diversity—and the risks of their extinction. Nearly all the languages belong to one of two major families, which are not mutually comprehensible. For example, two languages with similar names, Belanda Bor and Belanda Viri, spoken south and east of Wau, belong to separate families—a sign that these two groups have been pushed together by outsiders, but originate from different areas (Tucker, 1931, p. 54; Santandrea, 1964, p. 108). Some languages, such as Aja or Indiri, spoken in the Raga area, are small and probably unique to Western Bahr al-Ghazal. Others, such as Zande (spoken in Western Equatoria, CAR and the DRC) or the different Banda languages (spoken south of Raga and in CAR), have more speakers in other parts of Southern Sudan or Central Africa. And some are transnational languages from West Africa: two listed below are Hausa or Fulfulde. Njagulgule, a language spoken by very few people mainly in Raga town, is the same as the Darfurian language Beigo, which may now be extinct—Njagulgule people may have been Beigo clients in the past, and their leading family is of Beigo origin (Santandrea, 1964, p. 171). Gula (also called Kara), Binga and Yulu have speakers in CAR, but their origin narratives link them to Jebel Marra in Darfur.

Linguistic history indicates the changing meanings of the word Fertit. For historians of Darfur, the term comes from origin narratives of people linked to Darfur, who fled the assimilation, coercion or taxation of the Fur sultanate during its formation in the seventeenth century. In the south they became, in Fur terms, legitimate prey for the sultanate's slaving expeditions. The Njagulgule-Beigo language suggests this kind of history (O'Fahey, 1980, pp. 72ff). But R.S. O'Fahey's compelling and influential definition of Fertit does not account for the presence of West African and Central African languages in the area: speakers of these languages probably came as result of later wars and economic changes.

FIGURE 3.
SELECTED LANGUAGES SPOKEN BY PEOPLES IN WESTERN BAHR AL-GHAZAL STATE, LATE TWENTIETH CENTURY

Language	Language family	Number of speakers (studies conducted 1970–2000)
Aja	Nilo-Saharan	200
Bai	Niger-Congo	2,500
Banda, Banda	Niger-Congo	102,000 in CAR, some in Sudan
Banda-Mbrès	Niger-Congo	42,500 in CAR, some in Sudan
Banda, Mid-southern	Niger-Congo	
Banda, Ndele	Niger-Congo	35,500 in CAR, also in Sudan
Banda, Togbo-Vara	Niger-Congo	12,000 in DRC, CAR and Sudan
Banda West Central	Niger-Congo	7,500 in CAR and Sudan
Belanda Bor	Nilo-Saharan	8,000
Belanda Viri	Niger-Congo	16,000
Feroge	Niger-Congo	8,000
Fulfulde (also called Fulbe)	Niger-Congo	90,000 across Sudan
Gbaya (spoken by people called Kresh and Dongo)	Nilo-Saharan	16,000 in Bahr al-Ghazal and Darfur
Gula (also called Kara)	Nilo-Saharan	1,100
Hausa	Afro-Asiatic	80,000 across Sudan
Indiri	Niger-Congo	700
Mangayat	Niger-Congo	400
Ndogo	Niger-Congo	Few monolingual
Njagulgule	Nilo-Saharan	900
Shatt	Nilo-Saharan	15,000
Thuri	Nilo-Saharan	6,600
Togoyo	Niger-Congo	Extinct
Yulu	Nilo-Saharan	3,000
Zande	Niger-Congo	350,000 in Sudan

Source: Lewis (2009).

Lutfi Muhammad Wadatallah, a Kresh intellectual in Khartoum, reviews the linguistic origins of the term Fertit:

> I asked my father, he said, Fertit is strange. It's not in any
> of the languages of the Fertit tribes. But the origin itself is a
> matter of controversy. Some people say it refers to fruit eater.
> My father told me that this is the name given by Bornu to
> non-believers in God: Kresh, Binga and two others, four tribes
> using African traditional beliefs or *kujur* [Arabic, derogatory
> but widespread term for traditional beliefs]... Another piece
> of information, which is near to O'Fahey, *farru tihit* [Sudanese
> Arabic, 'they fled down'], people who were living in Jebel
> Marra and escaped [from Fur invasion]. But why not say it
> in Fur, why use an Arabic term? And if Fur were not in Jebel
> Marra where were they? If they are living together with Fur,
> there must be a common element. Not anything connects
> them with Fur now. I do believe these people were pagans.
> And I'm still looking for evidence that they were in Jebel
> Marra. All Fertit or certain tribes.[10]

Many people interviewed for this study offered, usually with a shy laugh, the 'fruit eater' explanation, often attributing it to their English teacher. For example, Ireneo Kunda, a Belanda chief, explains: 'Fertit—this name was named by English. It is not Fertit, it is called fruit eaters. Because we have so many fruits in forest.'[11] Although the use of the word long pre-dates British rule in the area, it may have connoted for British observers the hunter-gatherer livelihoods of forest people, or people on the run.

Categorizing Fertit people and their languages is a political act. Two groups sometimes described as Fertit, the Belanda Boor and the Shatt, both speak languages related to Luo, a Nilotic language spoken in

....

[10]   Interview with Lutfi Muhammad Wadatalla, intellectual from a Hofrat al-Nahas family, Khartoum, April 2010.

[11]   Interview with Ireneo Kunda, Belanda chief, Wau, 22 February 2010.

different variants across Sudan, and in Wau by people called Jur-Luo. British colonizers classed the Belanda Boor and the Shatt as Fertit and pushed them into the largely Fertit Western Bahr al-Ghazal. Shatt people lived on the border between the largely Nilotic flood plains and Raga county, and those who wanted to stay in Nilotic areas had to say that they were Shilluk (speakers of another Luo language). 'In Wau we are three Nilotic tribes, Shatt, Belanda Boor and Jur (Jur-Luo). Now they are all called Jur-Luo,' said one Shatt interviewee, Father Andrea Osman Okello.[12] In the years after the signing of the CPA, there was an increase in Jur-Luo consciousness in Wau, sometimes attributed to the appointment of a governor from that group. Some Shatt people on the border with the flood plain today are calling for their area of Raga county to be moved to the largely Nilotic Northern Bahr al-Ghazal.[13]

Histories of slavery

Fertit is a pejorative term undergoing a process of reclamation. Its negative connotations lie in the history of slavery in Fertit areas. Fertit does not mean slave but at one point it connoted 'enslaveable' in Darfur. Many Fertit people became Muslims, and some of these groups retained client status with Darfur groups who were once their patrons or masters long after the abolition of slavery. This openness to the culture and religion of former oppressors sometimes evinces suspicion among other southern groups. Understanding how slavery is interpreted is one way of understanding what it means to be Fertit. The interpretations presented here stress different themes: incorporation, victimhood, joking, resistance, clienthood, migration. These interpretations are attributed to individual interviewees who are identified by their ethnic group, but they do not necessarily reflect group views.

....

[12]   Interview with Fr Andrea Osman Okello, Vicar-General of Rumbek Diocese, Rumbek, 20 February 2010.

[13]   Interview, name and place withheld, 19 April 2009.

One characteristic of many powerful actors in the Bahr al-Ghazal's slaving systems was their ability to incorporate other groups as clients. Incorporation transformed both groups. The Fur sultanate needed slaves to build the terraces on Jebel Marra, but when provincial governors became too powerful, slaves were used to create a bureaucracy and army that could centralize power. Baggara groups used slaves as cultivators, giving them a food cushion that may have provided cattle-keepers with an insurance that allowed for greater participation in the riskier economy of pastoralism. Many powerful Baggara and Fur men made slave women into lower-status wives, whose different languages and cultures had a significant impact on the society (O'Fahey, 1980, p. 137). Mangayat people, captured by one of the Zande states, would marry within their group, and other Mangayat people even migrated to join them (Santandrea, 1953, p. 256). Some groups adopted leading families, who might be able to negotiate with powerful outsiders: the origins of the Feroghe leading family, for example, lie with a West African pilgrim, well-connected with the Fur sultan, who married a Kaligi chief's daughter and inherited from her father. Kaligi speakers are now called Feroghe. Such a historical origin story of a learned Muslim patriarch transforming a matrilineal African society is common across Sudan (Santandrea, 1964, pp. 143ff).

Some people have unforgiving recollections of the slave raiders, and describe slavery in terms of child abduction, or the trafficking of young women, reflecting the premium that slavers gave to youth and tractability. Suleiman Hussein Abdullahi, a Sara chief in Firga, just east of the border of the Kafia Kingi enclave, recalls the slave trade that was practiced in the early twentieth century. In 1916, the nominally independent sultanate of Darfur fell, and the turbulence of the time caused groups such as the Sara—with origin stories in Darfur and Central Africa—to flee to the Kafia Kingi enclave. 'Everyone was stealing children and bringing them to Dahal Koro [near Kafia Kingi] to the [slave] traders. They took the women too—our grandmothers who had come from El Fasher.'[14]

....

[14]   Interview with Suleiman Hussein Abdullahi, Sara chief, Firga, 21 March 2010.

For two groups with West African origin stories, slavery is a running joke. Fellata people (associated in Bahr al-Ghazal with a particularly nomadic form of cattle-keeping) and Bornu people (associated with trade and Islamic learning) have no history of slave raiding between them, but make jokes about capturing each other. They have an Arabic saying, *sidkum wa-abidkum* [your masters and your slaves], which several interviewees repeated with a laugh, but could not explain further.[15] Professor Amin Abu Manga of Khartoum University suggests that the joke is part of Nigerian humour too:

> *Sidkum wa-abidkum*—there was never slave raiding between
> Bornu and Fulani. In the time of *shaykh* Osman [dan Fodio,
> a nineteenth century Fulani leader] the Fulani subjugated
> the Bornu capital and the Bornu recaptured it after 40 days,
> maybe that's the origin of the joke.[16]

Some interviewees stressed the fighting capacity of their group, perhaps indicating a historical memory of resistance to coercion. For example, a Binga informant, asked to explain why his people had so many difficulties with the British, stated that Binga people were 'very, very wild. Why? They're wild. They don't want someone to rule them.'[17] A Kresh informant explained the meaning of the word, Naka—the name of a Kresh sub-grouping: 'Naka comes from a word for syphilis. It means, I'll tire you out like the clap.'[18]

Some Bahr al-Ghazal groups were recognized as clients of specific Baggara groups, doing dangerous or laborious jobs such as elephant

....

[15] Interviews with Mororo people and Bornu man in nomad camp near Magwe, Western Bahr al-Ghazal, March 2010; interview with Al-Amin Abu Manga, Director of Institute of Afro-Asian Studies, Khartoum University, Khartoum, April 2010.

[16] Interview with Al-Amin Abu Manga, Director of Institute of Afro-Asian Studies, Khartoum University, Khartoum, April 2010.

[17] Interview with Romano Ramadan Isma'il, member of the State Legislative Assembly, Wau, February 2010.

[18] Interview with Mohammed Wadatalla, member of parliament for a Western Bahr al-Ghazal constituency and member of the Border Commission, April 2010.

hunting, fighting or farming. They reportedly recognized the rights of their patron households over their children, and to *diya* (compensation due to victims) for their own injuries or death. They used the remoteness of the borderlands between Darfur and Southern Sudan to diversify their livelihoods and evade taxes. Bandala (or Mandala, or Ngbandala) was a name for one such Bahr al-Ghazal group of clients of the Habbaniya or Rizeigat, two of the largest Baggara tribes (Herbert, 1926, pp. 187ff). Bandala is now considered an offensive term. According to one Rizeigat tribal office holder: 'In 1920, [paramount chief] Ibrahim Musa Madibbo made a rule, if you said that word you would go to prison.'[19] Bandala people are now called Rizeigat (in this study, they are called Bahr al-Ghazal Rizeigat, because many of them live in the border zone, and come under the southern system of traditional authorities).

Clienthood was different from incorporation: it allowed for subordinate groups to negotiate with and sometimes flee from oppressors. Fertit interviewees from client groups often stressed their sense of historical agency, suggesting that the status afforded them certain possibilities. The Kara group, who are discussed at several points in this study, are a case in point. One Darfurian interviewee stated that before the Mahdiya, Kara people were seen as a Bandala group for the Taysha, the small Baggara tribe of the Mahdi's successor or Khalifa. But the Mahdiya emancipated them—the Khalifa publicly threw tribal genealogies into the river (Muhammad, 1982, p. 1). Kara interviewees in Minamba, Bahr al-Ghazal, and in the Kara club in Omdurman both stressed Kara military contribution to the Mahdiya. They presented a copy of Zulfo's book on the 1898 battle of Karari (when British machine guns defeated the Mahdist army), with a handwritten index of references to the part played by the Kara army, and annotations of the remarks of Winston Churchill (a Karari participant who later became a British prime minister) about the courage of the enemy: 'the bravest men that ever walked the earth, destroyed not conquered by machinery' (Zulfu, 1973, p. 335). All Kara

....

[19]   Interview with Muhammad Isa Aliyu, historian and Rizeigat official, Khartoum, 4 May 2010.

interviewees stated that Mahdist generals Ibrahim Khalil and Hamdan Abu Anja were both Kara.[20] Abu Anja captured and beheaded the Rizeigat chief Madibbo in El Obeid, and Madibbo called his captor a slave at his execution: 'I did not ask mercy of you, only justice, but a slave like you cannot be noble' (Holt, 1970, p. 154). It was an important moment in Sudanese history, when people from a violent periphery were challenging an older order—and becoming drawn into a powerful economic system based in Khartoum.

Links between Kara and Taysha groups still exist amongst border peoples: Ali Kushayb is a Taysha militia commander, reportedly with a Kara or Binga mother, who was indicted by the International Criminal Court (ICC) for crimes committed in Darfur in 2004. Court documents explain his lineage:

> Ali KUSHAYB was an 'Aqid al Oqada' (meaning 'colonel of colonels') in Wadi Salih Locality, in the state of West Darfur. By virtue of this tribal position, he was one of the most senior leaders in the tribal hierarchy in Wadi Salih Locality... From in or about August 2003, KUSHAYB commanded thousands of Militia/Janjaweed... KUSHAYB is about 50 years old. His father is from the Taisha tribe, while his mother is from a tribe from southern Sudan (International Criminal Court, 2007, pp. 32–33).

Fertit client chiefs may have won some freedom to select slaves from their own or other groups as a levy. But this freedom meant that the interests of leading families were set at odds with the slaves chosen,

....

[20]   Hamdan Abu Anja's southern origins are widely recognized (see Holt, 1970, p. 63). But the Kara origins of Ibrahim Khalil are not: Hill (1951, p. 174) and al-Hasan (1995, p. 189) both state that Khalil was the brother of a cousin or first cousin of the *khalifa* Abdullahi, who was from the Taysha group of Arabic-speaking Baggara. These accounts are not necessarily incompatible—Khalil may have had Kara as well as Taysha relatives. Some historians inadvertently downplayed or mistook the role of Bahr al-Ghazal groups in the Mahdiya: for example, the authoritative Holt identified Kara with the name of the fort where elite Mahdist troops from Southern Sudan were stationed, and described Abu Anja as a 'Mandala' or Bandala rather than Kara (1970, pp. 63, 135, 206, 214, 250, 260).

introducing a slavery-based hierarchy into Dar Fertit society. Lutfi Muhammad Wadatallah explains that people have been escaping from chiefs to cities since the nineteenth century:

> Some people escaped from the toughness of rulers and
> sometimes the chiefs in the area are very tough, if you do very
> minor crime you will be punished severely.[21]

For many people, slavery was the means by which they moved from rural to urban life. In most cases, this experience would have been deeply oppressive, but for some it provided opportunities. Stanislaus Abdullahi Paysama's memoir, *How a Slave Became a Minister* (nd), gives the most detailed written account of the early twentieth century trade. He was born in a village in South Darfur around 1904, the son of a Fur *faki* or Muslim spiritual leader. The nominally independent sultan of Darfur, Ali Dinar, was violently disciplining Baggara groups on the southern border at the time, and Paysama's abduction came in the context of these political disorders. He was captured when he was about ten years old and was taken to Kafia Kingi, where his captor died. In 1914 Kafia Kingi was under British control: slavery was officially abolished but not suppressed. He was captured again by a Fur slave dealer. Put in a room with two older Fur girls, he told them his story lying between them in their bed.

> They related to me the story of this man. His name was
> Abdullahi Abu Talatin, a slave dealer by profession. He bought
> or stole boys and girls and sold them. He brought them from
> here and made marks on their faces to change their features.
> He castrated some boys and sold them. 'See what he has
> done to us' [The girls have been disabled by the wooden foot
> restraints] (Paysama, nd, p. 33).

Paysama escaped the slave dealer and ended up in a government programme for freed slaves, which turned abducted boys into policemen

....

[21] Interview with Lutfi Muhammad Wadatalla, intellectual from a Hofrat al-Nahas family, Khartoum, April 2010.

BINGA HISTORY AND MIGRATIONS

The Khartoum Binga Association is led by Binga professionals, with jobs in private schools, clinics and government departments. It has a collection of maps and calligraphed display boards setting out the association's view of Binga history, for use at exhibitions. The display boards say that they are Muslims; that they are Negro Africans from a place near Jebel Marra; and that they lived in Diminga around 1445. Also called Dar Abo Diima, Diminga was the populous and mixed southernmost province of the Fur sultanate. The display boards are intended for Khartoum audiences: they stress African origins, but omit direct references to slavery, preferring to link their history with Darfur state elites. One of the display-panels lists the Binga generals (Ramadan Burra, Abd al-Mukarram) who fought with Ali Dinar against the British, and whose soldiers escaped to Kafia Kingi after his downfall. By contrast, in Minamba, near Raga, the Binga chief's account of history included slavery and displacement: he referred to a slave market in the Kafia Kingi enclave called Jebel Bio [they sold him], which functioned until 1920.* Other Binga historians stress Binga historical agency, their military achievements and early adoption of the musket. These histories are not incompatible: slavery transformed the societies of Bahr al-Ghazal, and brought people from the margins into military or marital hierarchies at the centre of the state.

The Binga Association's display boards are reminders of the importance of history for people who have undergone long migrations: an attempt by ordinary people to work out a sense of belonging in a society that has gone through two centuries of violent change. One Binga elder from the Umbelacha area explained places where Binga people belong:

> 'Binga places: Garsila, Chad, Sungo, Kafindebi, Minamba, Kafia Kingi, al-Fashir. The sultan of the Binga—Sultan Dahia in Minamba. He is the biggest one. He has a document from the English times... In Buram, in Habbaniya areas, they have an *umda*. They have *shaykhs* in Gar Sila and Nyala. In Fashir they follow the Fur. They don't have *shaykhs*... Binga in al-Fashir are now mixed up with the Fur... they don't speak the [Binga] language.'

> 'If you're a Binga person in al-Fashir without a *shaykh* and you don't speak Binga, what makes you Binga?'

> 'You say you are.'

* Interview with Binga chief Abbakr Abd al Rahman Dahia, Minamba, March 2010.

and abducted girls into police brides. But he was fortunate: he was taken to a missionary school in Wau and his education eventually enabled him to have a government career that culminated in a cabinet post. Paysama was someone whose experience of slavery turned him from Fur to Fertit. His memoir ends with his return to his mother's village as a government minister, where he found no relatives or friends, and where he decided to return to Wau. His experience of slavery was unusual in that it brought him dramatic and powerful opportunities.

Religious and political affiliation

Many Fertit people are Muslims, following both vernacular versions of Islam and versions inspired by the most prestigious ancient texts of the religion. Some Fertit ethnic groups associate their group practices with those texts—they are 'Islamized' as well as being Muslim. Roman Catholicism is also widespread (there are few Protestants) and many people follow traditional African religions. Religious diversity is apparent in marriage customs. Feroghe groups fast, pray, marry, divorce and inherit in accordance with textual versions of Islamic law, even though Islamic legal institutions for civil procedures such as inheritance do not exist in Bahr al-Ghazal.[22] Kresh and many other groups marry with a bride-wealth that comprises agricultural tools and the provision of agricultural labour (in the violent nineteenth century, Kresh dowries were firearms and ivory). Some people marry according to Islam, some according to Catholicism, some according to traditional African beliefs, and some according to a mixture of these faiths.

Relatively few Fertit Catholics receive the Eucharistic sacrament, mainly because their marriage practices do not follow Catholic religious law and, in contravening that aspect of the law, they would be committing sacrilege to take the consecrated bread and wine of the Eucharist.[23]

....

[22] Interview with Abdullahi Tamim Fartak, Feroghe chief, Raga, March 2010.

[23] Interviews with Father Paul Annis, Combonian missionary, February 2010; Catholic school teacher, name withheld; women's leader, name withheld, Raga, March 2010.

Sometimes, Catholics are in polygamous relationships recognized by African customary beliefs. And sometimes people are in 'come and stay' relationships, not regulated by customs or religious laws, but resulting from the social changes brought on by many decades of war and urbanization.

Many groups in the area practice female circumcision, which is sometimes associated with Islam or with Arab or urban culture and its notions of female respectability (however, it is not required by Islamic law and it widely exists in non-Muslim, non-Arab and non-urban cultures across Africa). Banda groups probably adopted the practice in Central Africa or during their time in Kafia Kingi, where they moved to escape Sanusi's slave raiding in the early twentieth century. Feroghe, Ngulgule, Kresh Hofra, Aja, Woro and Azande reportedly maintain the practice; but other groups, such as Bviri, Shatt and Mangaya, reject it (Santandrea, nd, pp. 42–52; Santandrea, 1980, p. 828).

In Sudan, the adoption of female circumcision or Islamic inheritance law by an ethnic or social group is often a cultural and political statement of affinity with the culture and politics of the northern Nile valley, the cultural heartland of the state. Adoption of these practices may have been the outcome of conviction or religious devotion, or it may be linked to strategies of client groups to identify with patrons. The political dimensions of the differences between vernacular Islam and state-endorsed versions were on display in Raga county during the 2010 general election campaign. Both NCP and SPLM presidential candidates visited the tiny electorate in Raga. In the south, the NCP candidate, President Omar al-Bashir, said little about his version of religion: widely associated with his party's justifications for their actions during the civil war, he may have calculated that it was unlikely to provide electoral advantage. But the SPLM candidate, Yasir Arman, appealed to Raga Muslims to be true to vernacular versions of Islam, in contrast to the rigorous textual versions that the SPLM associates with Islamist extremism and state corruption:

> Raga has northern and Southern dimensions, Raga people are
> border peoples... Raga Muslims have their own Islam, not the

Islam of the Taliban, of corruption. Anyone who has drunk
sorghum beer should not vote for Bashir.[24]

Powerful external actors seeking support in Western Bahr al-Ghazal
sometimes try to categorize Fertit groups around religion, in order to
create Fertit constituencies that fit into wider discussions about national
identity. Today, more Islamized groups—such as the Feroghe and Njagulgule—are schematized to align them with the NCP. Others—such as
the Kresh—are categorized as potential recruits for the southern cause.
Members of all groups, however, have fought on both sides of the civil
wars in the south. These schemas do not explain much. In the 2010
elections, for example, the SPLM fielded Muslims for senior posts and
the NCP fielded many Kresh Catholics—NCP Catholics introduced the
visiting President al-Bashir with the Apostles Creed and the Gloria, parts
of Catholic liturgy.

Past religious affiliations also indicate the difficulty of neat schemati-
zation. The more Islamized Feroghe groups fled Mahdist conscription,
but Kara groups, as mentioned above, made an enormous contribution
to the Mahdiya.[25] In the 1960s, Kara people in Bahr al-Ghazal joined
the Anyanya rebellion; in 1991, the Kara chief was killed by a Darfurian
Islamist who had joined the SPLM and was marching through their village
to invade Darfur. Some Kara people in Western Bahr al-Ghazal joined
pro-Khartoum militias in the 1990s. But a decade later, Kara people in
Darfur ended up fighting with the rebels in the war in Darfur.[26]

The referendum on the future status of Southern Sudan has turned
border areas like Dar Fertit into sites of fierce competition between the
two parties to the CPA. Groups of mixed or indeterminate political and
religious affiliation, such as those mentioned here, may find themselves

....

[24] Speech of SPLM presidential candidate Yasir Arman, Freedom Square, Raga, 23 March
2010.
[25] SAD/815/7/8; and interview with Abdullahi Tamim Fartak, Feroghe chief, Raga, March
2010.
[26] Interviews with Kara people in Minamba, 18 March 2010; and with Kara people in
Omdurman, 27 April 2010.

pulled into this struggle. The risk of such competition is highest in the Kafia Kingi enclave itself.

Fertit and Awlad Arab: groups living around the Kafia Kingi enclave

The population of the Kafia Kingi enclave is small. Estimates over the past 15 years range from 5,000 to 15,000.[27] Most people live along the Umbelecha and Adda rivers, and most are from Fertit groups (Hassan et al., 2005, p. 13). The British forcibly evicted the population of the enclave in 1930 as part of a policy that attempted to create a tangible division between 'Arab' and 'African' groups along the border. This policy, discussed at length in subsequent chapters, generated many tribal lists that showed the astonishing diversity and hybridity of the population of the enclave. Some people were pushed there by wars across Central Africa and the Sahel, others were drawn to participate in the lucrative slave trade, which lasted in the area until the 1920s.

When the British decided to clear Kafia Kingi in 1930, they classi-fied people as Awlad Arab, Fertit and sometimes Fellata. Awlad Arab [Arabic, 'sons of Arabs'] refers to groups who often shared origin narra-tives, languages and histories of clienthood with some Fertit groups, but who were seen as more Darfurian, more Arabized, or more Islamized. One official listed them in 1933 as Bornu (also known as Kanuri), Ronga (also known as Runga), Baghirma, Gimr, Dagu, Sara, Barta and Burgo (SDD/SCR/66-D-3). Several of these small populations bear the names of pre-colonial West African states, and they were sometimes lumped together as 'Fellata', a Sudanese word for West African Fulbe people often applied indiscriminately to any West African (B.G.P. 16.B.2).

Groups classed as Fertit also existed in the enclave. The British frequently reported on what they termed Bandala (or Bahr al-Ghazal Rizeigat) groups who used the area to evade taxes. Binga and Kara people

....

[27]   As noted above, the 5,000 figure is extrapolated from extracts of a report in Arabic on the drugs trade in Radom Biosphere Reserve, see footnote 4.

moved to the north of the Umbelacha River, and now many of them live around Songo. Yulu, Dongo and Kresh groups also live in the area. These people have origin narratives in Jebel Marra, links with languages spoken in Bahr al-Ghazal, Central Africa, and include followers of Islam, Christianity and traditional religions.

In the late 1990s, a study of Radom—the locality that administers the Kafia Kingi enclave—found that the groups described by the British as Awlad Arab are mostly living north of Radom town, on the Bahr al-Arab/ Kiir River, making a living from cultivation, livestock-keeping and trade. Binga and Kara people cultivate and hunt along the Umbelacha. But the enclave itself has been severely depopulated by endemic diseases, the

FIGURE 4.
PEOPLE LIVING AROUND THE KAFIA KINGI ENCLAVE

Tribe	Place of residence	Original homeland	Economic activity
Binga	Radom, Songo, Kafindebei	Kafia Kingi	Agriculture, hunting, honey-collection
Kara	Radom, Goz Shalal	Kafia Kingi	Agriculture, hunting, honey-collection
Dongo	Radom, Titripi	Jebel Dongo	Agriculture, hunting, honey-collection
Kresh	Radom, Kafia Kingi	Bahr al-Ghazal	Agriculture, hunting, honey-collection
Sara	al-Muraraya	Agriculture	
Bornu	Muraya, Radom	Agriculture	
Masalit	Dafag, Ilaybo	El Geneina, Gereida	Agriculture, trade
Fellata	al-Fifi	Tulus	Agriculture
Bagirma	Muraya	Agriculture	
Habbaniya	al-Hujayrat, al-Fifi	Agriculture	

Notes: Tribal groups are listed according to those that live along the Umbelacha and Adda rivers (1–4) and the Bahr al-Arab/Kiir River (5–10). All the settlements here are shown in Map 2 above.

Source: From a report on the drugs trade in the Radom Biosphere Reserve in the late 1990s, see footnote 4.

rigours of living in a heavily militarized border zone, and the expansion of the nature reserve, which displaced some villagers in 1990s, and imposes many rules on the economic life of the people in the area. 'Most of the population of Hofrat al-Nahas is now in Khartoum,' says former Western Bahr al-Ghazal governor Mark Nyipuoc.[28]

Non-Fertit groups to the north of the Kafia Kingi enclave

Radom town, just outside the north-eastern tip of the Kafia Kingi enclave, has much of the social and cultural diversity of the Kafia Kingi enclave. People recognize their links with the south, but identifying as Southerner or Fertit presents them with difficulties. One Radom resident who recognized and identified with the term Awlad Arab was asked if he wanted to be part of the south:

> My grandmother was a Southerner. But I don't want to go south. I think it's the property of the Nilotic tribes—Dinka, Nuer, Shilluk. Fertit are grade two in the south. People have Muslim names and they're considered grade two citizens. When it separates, the three tribes will rule it. There won't be peace and there will be oppression from those three tribes. They study the Ugandan syllabus. There won't be freedom for your culture. They hate anything northern, language or religion.[29]

British policy tried to create a racialized boundary between Arabs and Africans in these hybrid borderlands, which has echoes for its peoples today when wars in the south and in Darfur have increased sensitivity to ethnicity, and when the referendum on the future of the south may lead to the establishment of a new, ethnically-inflected dividing line in the area. Perceptions of that line are influenced by political affiliation—the

....

[28]   Interview with Mark Nyipuoc, SPLA lieutenant-general and governor of Western Bahr al-Ghazal state from 2006–09, March 2010.

[29]   Interview with Radom resident, name withheld, 7 November 2009.

speaker above is also an NCP politician—but they are interpreted in a personal way.

Some people may find it difficult to choose between south and north. British colonial officials found the Fellata—Fulbe-speaking West Africans—difficult to place. In the racial language of the day, they were less 'intermingled with black blood': Fellata men did not marry Fertit or Dinka women in the way that Rizeigat men did (SAD/735/4/1). In 1930, some were classed as Awlad Arab and sent to Darfur, while others were sent to eastern Sudan to work on agricultural schemes. Some are still in the south and those who are established citizens of Wau town meet the definition of a Southerner in the Interim Constitution of Southern Sudan.

> (a) any person whose either parent or grandparent is or was
> a member of any of the indigenous communities existing
> in Southern Sudan before or on January 1, 1956; or whose
> ancestry can be traced through agnatic or male line to any one
> of the ethnic communities of Southern Sudan; or
>
> (b) any person who has been permanently residing and
> whose mother and/or father or any grandparent have been
> permanently residing in Southern Sudan as of January 1, 1956
> (GoSS, 2005, Article 9.3).

The question of indigeneity will be very salient during the run up to the referendum in Sudan, which uses this constitutional definition as the basis of voter eligibility. The question will be very difficult to answer for some Fertit, along with other groups living on the border. Some Fellata individuals from Radom (in Darfur) and Wau hold senior ranks in the Sudan People's Liberation Army (SPLA), the army of Southern Sudan. Some Fellata groups can be recognized as Southerners by residence, but others are part-time, nomadic residents, moving through the Kafia Kingi enclave and Bahr al-Ghazal in search of dry season pasture.

The Mbororo Fellata are the most nomadic of all these groups. Mbororo cattle-keepers travel as far south as Equatoria, following the westernmost, tsetse-infested routes where other pastoralists will not risk their cattle. They can overcome these risks because of their cattle-keeping skills and because, unlike other pastoralist groups, they invest some of their surplus income in veterinary medicines. Their choice of route is most likely dictated by their political weakness relative to the large Baggara tribes such as the Rizeigat and Habbaniya, whose migratory routes lie to the east of the Kafia Kingi enclave and its tsetse flies.

In spite of their political weakness, Mbororo Fellata are sometimes presented as a threat. During the 1983–2005 civil war some supported the government side, and their familiarity with the area's terrain may cause anxieties in the SPLA. In a speech in Raga in March 2010, Southern Sudanese president Salva Kiir conflated Mbororo people with the Lord's Resistance Army (LRA), a Ugandan armed group whose leadership has been indicted by the International Criminal Court for crimes against humanity:

> Here you have LRA, here you have Mbororo, we don't
> consider them enemies to the people of Sudan, we consider
> them criminals. They bring their cows and don't feed them
> grass, they feed them cultivated grain. When they fight,
> they kill people. They must eat the forest grass and not take
> people's honey.[30]

The president's remarks came a few months after an alleged LRA attack in Boro Medina, near the Kafia Kingi enclave, which led to the deployment of a Ugandan army detachment in the area (Uganda has an agreement with the Government of Southern Sudan (GoSS) that allows it to deploy its troops in areas of suspected LRA activity). Some Fellata people interviewed cautiously expressed scepticism about the existence of the LRA in the area, suggesting that the spectre of this terrifying armed group has been invoked to justify militarizing the area. They reported a number of incidents when their young men and their cattle had been attacked

....

[30]   Speech of President Salva Kiir, Freedom Square, Raga, 23 Mar 2010.

by the SPLA—some of these allegations are being investigated by local authorities.[31]

Figure 4 above includes the Habbaniya, a Baggara or cattle-keeping group that is listed as agriculturalist. This is one of the most powerful political communities in South Darfur: the Kafia Kingi enclave and most south-western areas of South Darfur come under the Habbaniya *nazir* or paramount chief. But Baggara groups are currently undergoing many changes. Habbaniya and Rizeigat cattle-keepers still spend dry seasons in the eastern part of Raga county, usually going only as far as the Boro River, which runs 100–150 km south of the Bahr al-Arab/Kiir River. Many others from these groups are turning to farming, partly in response to taxes and the economic stresses of the war in Darfur: taxes on animals are significantly higher than those on crops, and since the 2003 outbreak of war in Darfur, livestock prices have been very volatile (Klugman and Wee, 2007, pp. 199–204). The water and land resources of the borderlands have attracted Baggara people to agriculture, sometimes in a nomadic style. One SPLA soldier from a Baggara group explains:

> Baggara people don't want problems. Their main activity was livestock, now it's agriculture, people have moved towards agriculture. Kuru between Timsah and the border is a grain exporting area—between six and 40 lorries a week to El Daien and Nyala. Raga people also import from Kuru. The farmers come in April and May [at the start of the rains], sow and return. You can't cross the Bahr al-Arab/Kiir when it is high. Most go home and return at harvest. The change to agriculture is very important.[32]

Today, farming is a cash activity, growing in status and importance, and the border zone is a place where pastoralists can become farmers. In the

....

[31]   Interviews with Fellata representatives, names and locations withheld; interview with SPLM local official, name and location withheld, March–April 2010.

[32]   Interview with Darfurian soldier from the SPLA, name and place withheld, March 2010.

past, Baggara groups incorporated Fertit groups from the south through slavery and other forms of coercion, often giving them agricultural tasks. The sorghum they cultivated may have given Baggara pastoralists more freedom to pursue riskier cattle-keeping livelihoods, as mentioned above. The shift in livelihoods is changing the status of cultivators, a reminder of the adaptability of Baggara social organizations. According to Muhammad Isa Aliyu, a historian and office bearer on the Rizeigat council, some people of slave lineage have become *umdas* [Arabic, tribal leaders]. And becoming Baggara is straightforward, only requiring a commitment to the principle of collective tribal payment of *diya* fines for the criminal liabilities of any Rizeigat individual or group:

> If you say I want to become Rizeigat, they say, choose your
> tribal section. Many people who join go to the nazir's house
> [section of the paramount chief] for protection. The *only*
> condition is that you commit to the diya. The chief won't even
> mention religion or marriage.[33]

For some people in Raga county incorporation into Baggara groups implies a rejection of origins and language, and has reminders of a servile past. But the adaptability of Baggara and Fertit social organizations may also be a resource.

There are few people from Nilotic groups who are permanent residents of Raga county and the Kafia Kingi enclave. Those who have moved there do not keep cows, although cattle-keeping is central to Dinka culture. Nearly all of them are involved in fishing or trade. Unlike Dinka people in the flood plains, they do not exchange cattle wealth at marriage. There are also many Dinka and Nuer soldiers in the SPLA contingents in Raga county, and in other security forces there.

Like Baggara groups, and like pre-colonial Sudanese states, Nilotic groups assimilate outsiders through marriage and other systems. But Dinka assimilation of Fertit people sometimes generates anxieties

....

[33] Interview with Muhammad Isa Aliyu, historian and Rizeigat official, Khartoum, 4 May 2010.

amongst the Fertit. 'Fertit are cheap,' sighed one Belanda woman, refer-
ring to the fact that Nilotic men can marry Fertit women without a cattle
bridewealth.[34] A number of tensions between Dinka and Fertit groups
emerged in the 1970s, discussed in Chapter 8 below. These tensions have
inflected the meaning of the word Fertit: for many people across Sudan,
and especially in parts of the south, it can now mean a Southerner who
is not Dinka.

Until the mid-twentieth century, the land to the north of the Umbelacha
River had a very sparse population comprising a few pastoralists and
Kara and Binga fugitives from the 1930 destruction of Kafia Kingi. But
the arrival of borehole technology in the 1960s changed the agricultural
possibilities of the area, at a time when drought hit Darfur. In 1973,
the state helped pastoralist groups from North Darfur resettle in Goz
Dango (also called al-Goz al-Gharbi, or the Goz Dango), the area of sandy
soils to the north of the Kafia Kingi enclave. Most of these people were
Zaghawa—speakers of a Nilo-Saharan language associated with sheep
and camel pastoralism in the semi-arid belt of North Darfur and Chad.
They established themselves in areas that had been very underpopulated and farmed on lands that belonged to Habbaniya people, gradually
acquiring land rights. In the 1980s a much more serious drought, which
coincided with a time of great international economic pressure on Sudan,
brought new groups of people to the area including Masalit, Masalati,
Gimir, Tama, Erenga and Misseriya Jebel—Darfurian groups mostly from
the Chadian border, and mostly speaking Nilo-Saharan languages in
addition to Arabic.[35] The droughts reshaped the population of the area
so that it came to reflect the diversity of Darfurian society as well as that
of Southern Sudanese and Central Africa. Displaced pastoralists used the
land and water resources of the area to change to a new livelihood.

In spite of a peaceful and productive start, many of these people were
caught up in the violence of the war in Darfur that began in 2003 and

[34] Interview with Belanda woman, name and place withheld, March 2010.
[35] Interview with Mohamed Ali, Nyala citizen, 6 Apr 2010.

aimed at reconfiguring the ethnic geography of the whole region. The Kara and Binga people who had lived there since 1930, and had some claim to the area as a homeland, were caught up in this violence too.

The term Fertit may have been invented by hostile outsiders, but it is sometimes now used by Fertit people themselves to describe their hybridity, their fluency with different cultures and languages, their life of displacement from savannah villages to towns in northern and Southern Sudan, and their fears of subordination or engulfment by neighbouring cultures perceived as more powerful—Fur, Arab or Dinka. These neighbours have come through the same wars, with similar turbulence; many Dinka, Fur and Baggara people also have to grapple with hybridity and subordination, a part of most Sudanese people's experience. But for a number of reasons, the large-scale, pastoralism-influenced Dinka and Baggara cultures are routinely presented as more homogenous, or introverted, or intractable, or self-assured than others. Evidence from the borderlands along the Bahr al-Arab/Kiir River suggests that they are also places where people from these powerful cultures can experiment with new kinds livelihoods, and practice being adaptable.

In the past, the Bahr al-Arab/Kiir River served as a border between enslaveable stateless people and the state, or between distinct cultural spheres that were deemed to be African or Arab. But it is also a border of interconnections and diversity, a place full of historical precedents for mutual understanding and potentially for cooperation. This chapter has reviewed a great many interpretations of these historical precedents because they are not well known and yet are likely to shape the responses of different groups to the possibility that the line between Darfur and the south will become a border in international law. The next chapter will show how a colonial attempt to abolish the flexibility of the border failed.

5. The 1930–46 Southern Policy: drawing a cultural and religious border

Decades of war and displacement helped bring about the depopulation of the Kafia Kingi enclave. The Anglo-Egyptian Southern Policy accelerated that displacement through its attempt to create clear cultural divides in an area of great hybridity, partly in response to a political crisis. The nineteenth century border between enslaveable fugitive or client populations and the state was concretized as a line between northerners and 'locals', Arabs and non-Arabs, Muslims and non-Muslims.

How did the Southern Policy come about? In 1924 the White Flag League, a proto-nationalist movement whose leadership was drawn from army officers of urban slave lineage, sought Egyptian support in Khartoum to challenge British power. In response, the British swiftly reduced the Egyptian presence in Sudan, and sought allies in rural Sudan, reworking traditional structures of power and restricting movement between different tribal groups. This entrenched a process of administrative devolution that had already begun a few years previously. In court, some of these White Flag League nationalists refused to respond when required to state their tribe, frightening the British into believing that nationalists were creating political communities that could rival British power (Vezzadini, 2008, p. 289). In northern Sudan, the British created or expanded local chiefly hierarchies, called Native Administration, with wide-ranging executive and judicial powers. In the south and culturally contiguous areas like the Nuba Mountains, they created a system of closed districts and internal passes, which almost completely cut these areas off from the north. A 1930 memorandum on Southern Policy set out its aims:

> The policy of the Government in the Southern Sudan is to
> build up a series of self-contained racial or tribal units with
> structures and organisation based, to whatever extent the
> requirements of equity and good government permit, upon
> indigenous customs, traditional usage and beliefs (Beshir,
> 1968, p. 115).

This policy presented administrators in Western Bahr al-Ghazal with a number of problems. First, the area had too many 'racial or tribal units', requiring expensive courts to base so-called 'good government' on 'indigenous custom'. These units were spread out thinly across a vast terrain, administered by one or two British political staff (B.G.P. 16.B.2, p. 7). British administrators could not cover their costs (made harder at a time when Sudan's revenues were badly affected by a crisis in its cotton industry, which was compounded by a global financial crisis) (Roden, 1974, p. 506). Second, the diversity and hybridity of Western Bahr al-Ghazal posed a challenge, as its people were seen to be open to outside influences.

R.G.C. Brock, then governor of Bahr al-Ghazal, set out examples of northern influence in a 1930 report to the Civil Secretary in Khartoum: becoming a Muslim was an informal condition for joining the police; chiefs wore Muslim dress; attachment to Islam was weakening attachments to tribal law; and half the population spoke Arabic at home. Raga's adoption of Arabic contrasted with other areas of the south (a contemporary report estimated that only 0.5 per cent of Dinka people could speak any Arabic at all) (ND/SCR/1/C/1). Some groups sponsored Islamic schools or practiced female circumcision. Brock saw these practices as 'a form of snobbery', an attempt to import foreign prestige into societies that he was trying to subordinate through a kind of neo-primordialism—a policy of trying to reinvent a fast-changing, open society as a closed, unchanging and archaic one.

The Kafia Kingi enclave, on the Darfur border, was a focus of attention for the Southern Policy. The British estimated that there were 2,575 taxpayers in the area in 1930 (they soon realized this was an underestimate). Five hundred were Fellata (also called Awlad Arab) and 800 Bandala or Bahr al-Ghazal Rizeigat—both groups that the colonial government saw as vectors of northern influence and as difficult to classify or administer. Both were also associated with the still-functioning slave trade, which in turn was associated with northern, Muslim and Arab penetration.[36]

In Wau, the British governor Brock decided on drastic implementation measures for the Southern Policy—measures that generated a great deal of work for officials in Darfur, causing controversy in Khartoum (Collins, 1983, pp. 176–89). Brock's administration abolished the town of Kafia Kingi, creating a no man's land along the south of the border (covering a wider area than the Kafia Kingi enclave of today). Bahr al-Ghazal authorities forbade the entry of 'all natives of Darfur and Kordofan', turning a cultural borderland into a barrier (B.G.P./SCR/I.C.6). (In 1931 the Brock Line, described further in Chapter 6, provided a permanent exception for Baggara pastoralists). Elsewhere in Bahr al-Ghazal many people were living far from the Arab or Muslim influences of Kafia Kingi, in 'self-contained racial or tribal units' (Beshir, 1968, p. 115) along rivers—possibly a nineteenth century strategic response to the new kind of slave raiding that targeted Bahr al-Ghazal's interior. But Brock wanted to change this too: the Southern Policy determined that they would all be moved from the river valleys and villages across the province to a 265-mile-long road from Wau to the western border town of Said Bandas (next to present day Boro Medina). They would be grouped roughly by language or origin and their many chiefs would come under four or five paramount chiefs and courts. British administration would penetrate more deeply; labour discipline would be instilled through road works to improve the existing track. Wage labour would start to spread in largely unmonetized societies. Disease control would improve (Reining, 1966, p. 101).

....

[36] B.G.P. 16.B.2, pp. 4–5; interview with chief Sulayman Husayn Abdullahi, Sara and other tribes in Firga, Firga, March 2010.

Memories of forced displacement

The displacements of this period were distinctive because they were linked explicitly to a cultural policy. But they also coincided with another major historical shift: the extension of state reach, brought about by the beginnings of lorry transport in Southern Sudan. This extension changed the relationship between the government centres in the towns and the mobile, adaptable populations of the countryside. These two forces of change in the 1930s—the Southern Policy and the rise of motor transport—are still within the living memory of Raga's oldest citizens. Their perceptions of the displacement that these changes caused provide an insight into an older world, before state-evasion became impossible.

People born after 1930 often assessed the displacements of that year positively, as a time when rural people first gained access to the social services of the town. Ireneo Kunda, a Belanda chief in Wau born some years later, dates the spread of education to 1930.

> When did people start to get educated? Around 1930–31.
> Before that people were not living on the road. But it existed,
> but no cars... Belanda people were eager for education and
> the [Catholic] mission school began in Deim Zubeir in 1930.[37]

But older people, who recalled the way of life before motor transport and urban services, remembered the coercion of 1930 with some bitterness: 'Up to now we are not glad,' said Lino Bianca, a Raga historian and language expert who was 15 at the time. Place names from this time are also reminders: at Katta, just east of Said Bandas, there was a settlement called Jabarona, a Sudanese Arabic word meaning 'they forced us'—a still current name for a settlement of displaced people (there are Jabaronas today in Omdurman and Juba). Nearby Lilli, a village for Kresh people moved from Hofrat al-Nahas, is a Kresh (or Gbaya) word for tsetse fly (it is now largely deserted but still infested). Sopo, a town for Kafia Kingi

....

[37]   Interview with Belanda chief Ireneo Kunda, Wau, February 2010.

Banda people on the road from Raga to Deim Zubeir, is a word for the crack of a whip in Banda languages.[38]

When the Bahr al-Ghazal provincial administration cleared the enclave, they moved about 27,000 men, women and children (5,457 taxpayers), most of whom were classed as Awlad Arab (a mix of Arabized or Islamized groups from West Africa or Darfur). Wau, once the provincial capital, had 1,553 taxpayers in 1937 (B.G.P./SCR/8-A-3; SAD/710/20, p. 20). The enclave also had more than 2,000 Kara and Binga people, who were required to move to the road from Boro Medina to Raga. Their origin narratives link them to Darfur as well as Central Africa, but they were perceived by the British as groups of slave status. The different versions of their origin narratives are worth examining as an example of how the British approach to clearing groups out of Kafia Kingi did not allow for ambiguous or hybrid ancestry.

Father Stefano Santandrea, the missionary linguist who is the main written source for the ethnology of the area, believed that they came from the eastern borders of what was then French Equatorial Africa (FEA), but admits that he had not met many Kara elders (Santandrea, 1964, pp. 229ff). Kara people have a well-documented history of involvement in the Mahdist movement and links to the Taysha, a Baggara group that was also deeply involved in the Mahdiya. Kara and Binga people interviewed for this study believe that they came originally to Kafia Kingi from Darfur, often dating their move to the fall of the Darfur sultanate in 1916 or a few years before that.[39]

In Jebel Marra, colonial officials described the existence of Kara speakers, who called themselves Karanga. In Diminga (also called Dar Abo Diima), the populous and mixed southernmost province of the Fur sultanate, colonial officials reported that there were Binga speakers called Tebella: one early twentieth-century traditional leader described

[38] Interview with Pancracio Mbali Yango, MP for Sopo; and with former Lilli resident, February and March 2010.

[39] Interviews with Kara and Binga people, Raga, Minamba, Nyala, Omdurman and Khartoum, March–May 2010.

the difference between Fur and Binga as a difference between leaders (*shartais* in Fur language) and 'common villagers' (MacMichael, 1922, p. 97). British officials sometimes depicted Binga and Kara people as former slaves or clients of Darfurian groups such as the Taysha, although Binga and Kara self-perceptions are more historically nuanced.

There were also links to today's CAR. A French explorer reported that a major slave raiding expedition of the Fur sultanate in 1840 crossed Binga lands south of Wadai (Bizemont, quoted in O'Fahey, 1980, p. 138). Officials were also aware of French reports of Kara and Binga people in Ouanda Jallé, an area of eastern FEA, during the slave raids of Rabih Fadlallah, at the end of the nineteenth century.[40]

Binga and Kara people could have been described as Darfurian, but the British decided to move them to Minamba, a village on the road between Raga and Boro Medina. Perhaps this was because the British associated Binga and Kara people with slave lineage, and they believed that Southern Policy would protect people from slavery—the continuing slave raiding around Kafia Kingi was one reason for its closure. One thousand Binga (about 200 taxpayers) and 700 Kara (140 taxpayers) refused to move, and a British official named S.R. Simpson burnt them out (B.G.P./SCR/8-A-3). Not only their houses were destroyed but also their grain stores. In the phrase of one group of Kara interviewees this was 'the time of wars'.[41]

They fled to the northern bank of the Umbelacha River, where more than two hundred died of starvation the next year as a result of the destruction of their grain stores.[42] Bahr al-Ghazal administrators remorselessly pursued their policy, pushing their colleagues to burn them out of their new homes in order to move them to Minamba. Following this episode British administrators in Darfur accused their southern counterparts of using state terror against the people. Binga and Kara groups spent

---

[40] 'Historical note on the Kara', nd, no attribution. Andrew Baring papers, unclassified.

[41] Interview with Kara people, Minamba, March 2010.

[42] SDD/SCR/66-D-3: the memo states that 194 deaths were listed, but that the real number was 238. However, the '2' in 238 could be read as a '3'.

six recalcitrant years on the northern side of the border before a letter
from the civil secretary in Khartoum gave them leave to remain. Bahr
al-Ghazal administrators thereupon tried to prevent them from visiting
their relatives across the border (Collins, 1983, p. 264).

The refugees from the Kafia Kingi enclave were eventually slotted
into the Darfur Native Administration, coming under the nazir of the
Habbaniya tribe, a Baggara group whose lands covered the south-west
edge of Darfur, and who were, for tax purposes, the second largest group
in South Darfur. The Habbaniya nazir appointed the 'umda for the mixed
population of Radom, and he currently has the power to appoint the
'umdas and shaykhs of the Kafia Kingi enclave.[43]

The Southern Policy and Islam

Limiting the powers and spread of Islam in Bahr al-Ghazal was an aim of
Southern Policy that is still remembered by Muslim people in Raga today.
One of the largest groups in the district is the Feroghe, who were born
out of an alliance between a Bornu pilgrim and a group called Kaligi, and
were scattered across the borderlands between the Boro River (that runs
from Said Bandas to Boro) and the Bahr al-Arab/Kiir River. The British
feared that the presence of Fellata groups in the area was leading Feroghe
people to adopt stricter versions of Islam:

> The Feroge, though perhaps not a strictly Mahommedan
> tribe as stated in the Bahr El Ghazal Handbook, are rapidly
> becoming so, owing to the RAGA Fallata being under the
> Feroge chief who is a devout Moslem (B.G.P. 16.B.2, pp. 5–6).

Isa Fartak, the Feroghe chief, wrote letters to the British authorities, in
precise classical Arabic, asking permission for schools and mosques to

[43] Interviews with Miskin Musa Abd al-Mukarram, Executive Director of Timsah payam,
March 2010; and Ibrahim al-Amin Ali, Kara 'umda of Radom, April 2010

be built.[44] His willingness to confront the British led to his dismissal and imprisonment in Equatoria: according to Abdullahi Tamim Fartak, the present-day chief, he was moved to al-Fashir because he was teaching other prisoners the Quran.[45]

In Raga, in 1930, British views of Islam were no less confused than they are in the UK today: it was associated with contamination and fanaticism; there was a fear of 'strict' versions of religion and the possibility that Islam might spread troublesome aspirations or 'snobbery' among Southerners. British policy discouraged Arabic language and Islam, and even included the burning of white *jallabiya* robes associated with Arab culture (B.G.P. 16.B.2). One British district commissioner who was a particularly keen observer of male fashion issued the following order in 1935:

> I notice that in spite of frequent requests to the contrary, large quantities of 'Arab' clothing are still being made and sold. Please note that, in future, it is FORBIDDEN to make or sell such clothes. Shirts should be made short with a collar and opening down the front in the European fashion and NOT an open neck as worn by the Baggara of Darfur. Also tagias [i.e., head cover] as worn by Arabs to wind emmas [i.e., turbans] round are not to be sold in future. No more Arab clothing is to be made as from today; you are given till the end of February to dispose of your present stock. This order applies to all outside agents and owners of sewing machines.[46]

The ferocious interpretation of Southern Policy in the district may have been partly to do with the personalities involved, whose angry correspondence sometimes suggests they had an emotional investment in repressing the area's diversity and openness to outside influence.

....

[44]   Some of these letters are reproduced at the end of Sikainga (1983).

[45]   Interview with Feroghe chief 'Abdullahi Tamim Fartak, Raga, March 2010.

[46]   Letter from Raja District Commissioner to Mr Emmanuel Lagoteris, Agent of Messrs. Papoutsidis at Raja, January 21st, 1935, quoted in (Abdel Rahim, 1966, p. 234).

The afterlife of Southern Policy

The 1930 Southern Policy was short-lived. It was reversed in 1946 when the British, contesting Sudan's future with Egypt, reincorporated the south into northern administration, as part of a strategy aimed at supporting and enlarging anti-Egyptian constituencies. But the policy resonated for a long time afterwards. Following independence, when divisions between Southern Sudan and the central government led to civil war, nationalist historians from the Khartoum elite wrote about the British repression of Arab and Islamic culture, in order to stress the colonial roots of the civil war (Abdel Rahim, 1966, pp. 227–49; Beshir, 1968, p. 52). British files from the period were distributed amongst (northern Sudanese) government personnel in the south in the belief that this would promote unity.[47]

However, the 1930 policy finds endorsement today from some Southern nationalists. One GoSS official who was interviewed for this study praised it:

> Some people may blame the British administration, but the
> British helped in some way. If there were no closed districts
> the penetration [of Islam] would have been more.[48]

For some Muslims in Raga, Southern Policy reminds them of a time when their religion was seen as a threat to southern political order. Some senior officers in the SPLA may still share this view:

> SAF [the Sudan Armed Forces, or government army] wants
> to change the demography of [Western Bahr al-Ghazal]. The

....

[47] A collection of these documents was published without any bibliographic information under the title *British Southern Policy in the Sudan*. A brief introduction states: 'The following documents from the Government archives of Khartoum were mimeographed and distributed by the Sudan Government for the use of the Arab officers in the Southern question propaganda. (There are more documents on the Southern Sudan policy which were not duplicated as unfit for the purpose.) Copies of these documents were taken from a government office in Equatoria by a Southern patriot who later escaped to one of the neighbouring African countries.'

[48] Interview with GoSS official, name withheld, Juba, March 2010.

> Government of Sudan manipulated our centre of gravity, the
> unity of the south. From day one [of the civil war], the north
> set foot in Raga. Some tribes like Kresh and Feroghe because
> of their religion are a part of the north. Kresh and Feroghe are
> Muslims, if you are Muslim you are assumed to be an Arab.[49]

SPLA views are not uniform: the southern army has senior officers who
are Muslims and northerners. The SPLA reflects some of the contradictions in SPLM policy towards Islam, which has inherited and created
all-south Islamic institutions but does not yet have a clear set of roles for
them. Many Raga Muslims follow the developments in Islamic policy and
fear any association of their religion with threats to national security.

Long discarded, the 1930–46 Southern Policy still clearly has an
afterlife. Having turned the border into a cultural barrier—a boundary
between Africans and Arabs—it remains a living political tool. Culture
had always been an element defining the border, alongside ecological and
economic elements: Southern Policy made culture decisive as it aimed
to cut off relations between the two culturally distinct populations that
it was trying to create.

The belief in the value of maintaining cultural distinctness, and the
focus on mistrust and injustices between different cultural groups,
detracts from an understanding of the shared possibilities and shared
experiences of exploitation across cultures. The cultural border is still a
powerful part of political and security calculations of both sides today.
Some important groups believe that the notion of unbridgeable cultural
differences implied in the 1930–46 Southern Policy reflects reality and
seek an emphatic Afro-Arab border. The next chapter looks at some of
those political and security calculations, presenting a political history of
the border from pre-colonial times to the present day.

....

[49]   Interview with senior SPLA officer, name and location withheld, June 2010.

6.   Delineations: the political border

In the pre-colonial era, the southern border of Darfur was defined by a set of migrations and encroachments rather than a line or a river. Darfurian hunters, pastoralists, slavers and tax-collectors all had southern limits to their activities, but these limits shifted with the seasons, or in response to foreign markets and empires, or ecological and cultural change. 'Dar Fertit, the other side of the frontier, was always on the move, it was not so much a place but rather a state of mind,' wrote O'Fahey (1982, p. 82). Borders marked notions such as enslaveability and ecological shifts rather than lines on a map.

This chapter looks at the development of political borders since that time. It presents evidence from archive sources on the understandings of the border between Darfur and the south under each regime since the nineteenth century.

Border delineation from the pre-colonial period to the Mahdiya

One of the earliest written references to Darfur's political borders comes in Muhammad ibn Umar al-Tunisi's record of his visit to Darfur and Wadai in the early nineteenth century. In 1811, al-Tunisi noted that the sultans of pre-colonial Wadai and Darfur erected iron spikes to mark their borders (O'Fahey, 1980, p. 82). Darfur's borders with Wadai and Kordofan were contested, and some political effort may have gone into their delimitation. But al-Tunisi's map of Darfur does not even show the Bahr al-Arab/Kiir River and he does not mention it as a border: 'To the south, Darfur ends with the empty spaces between it and Dar Fertit' (al-Tunisi, n.d., p. 136). Political structures changed at the border: border peoples such as the Feroge, Dajo, Bina [probably Binga] each had their own chief, subject to the sultan in al-Fashir, rather than a Fashir-appointed administrator (Santandrea, 1964, p. 167).

During the Turkiya (1821–82), when Bahr al-Ghazal was overrun by private proxies of the new state in Khartoum, the southern military threat changed the nature of the border and the political life of border people. Zubeir Pasha, one of the most important proxies in Bahr al-Ghazal, says in a memoir recorded by a British officer in Cairo that he 'reigned over the country and all the adjoining territory as far as the Bahr el Arab', which is an indication of the Turkiya border. But in the same memoir, he indicates that Hofrat al-Nahas copper mines at the far northern edge of the Kafia Kingi enclave 'were considered to be in Dar Fur' and not Bahr al-Ghazal (Jackson, 1913, pp. 30–35). O'Fahey also puts Hofrat al-Nahas as the southern limit of the sultanate, his sources implying that Darfurian slave raids did not venture very much farther south (O'Fahey, 1980, p. 137).

In 1874, Zubeir invaded Darfur from Bahr al-Ghazal and defeated the Fur sultanate. Four days after Zubeir's arrival in the Darfur capital, El Fasher, the Turkiya governor-general arrived from Khartoum. Zubeir claimed that he had conquered the sultanate on behalf of the Egyptian ruler, thus establishing the Turkiya claim to Darfur, incorporating Darfur into Turkiya Sudan, and making the southern border of Darfur into a provincial border (Ibrahim, 2008, p. 9). Writing after Zubeir's subsequent defeat, Gessi, the penultimate Turkiya governor of Bahr al-Ghazal, equivocally delimited his province's northern border along the Bahr al-Arab/Kiir River:

> The Bahr-el-Arab marks the limit separating Darfour from the
> Bahr-el-Ghazal provinces... the stations to the south of the
> river, were also subject to the ancient sultan of the realm...
> Properly speaking, I ought to say that no central government
> existed there. The country was divided among the greatest
> chiefs who commanded the provinces dependent on them...
> The Sultan of Darfour never meddled with the internecine
> quarrels of his vassals. It was enough if they paid their tribute
> regularly; he cared for nothing else (Gessi, 1892, p. 297).

The Mahdiya (1882–98) briefly set up a province or *amala* in Bahr al-Ghazal and (more permanently) in Bahr al-Jebel, near present day Juba. It did not have effective control of Bahr al-Ghazal: the Mahdist commander was sent to Darfur in 1885 to deal with a revolt by Baggara groups, and left the area exposed to Belgian incursions in Hofrat al-Nahas (1894), and French incursions in Bahr al-Ghazal and Upper Nile (1898). The non-Arab people of the South Darfur border were known as *ahl al-sudan*, or Sudan people, to distinguish them from Arab Baggara—an indication that the Mahdist frontier was a cultural one, and that the notion of cultural enslaveability survived the Mahdiya (al-Hasan, 1995, pp. 30–31).

The border between Anglo-Egyptian Sudan and the sultanate of Darfur, 1898–1916

The British-dominated Anglo-Egyptian regime (1898–1955) rapidly took control of the south after defeating the Mahdiya. Mainly for financial reasons, the British initially decided to restore Darfur's nominal independence, recognizing Ali Dinar, a member of the Fur sultanate's ruling family, as a sultan paying tribute to the new regime in Khartoum (Theobald, 1965, p. 30). In 1898 the Khartoum government declared the Bahr al-Arab/Kiir River to be the southern border of Darfur, but it did not have effective control over the area, and nor, apparently, did it explain the borders to the new tributary sultan of Darfur (GoS, 2008, p. 187). In 1899 Ali Dinar wrote to the governor-general saying that El Hufra (Hofrat al-Nahas), El Kara and all the west belongs to Darfur' (Theobald, 1965, p. 35). Two years later he asked for Egyptian and British flags that he could fly at Hofrat al-Nahas, by which he intended to show his *own* claim to the area, as an Anglo-Egyptian tribute payer. In 1903, the sultan sent a protest to Khartoum about the first British expedition to Hofrat al-Nahas. It was not until 1911 that the governor-general informed Ali Dinar, without much clarity, what his southern borders would be:

> As regards your request to define the boundaries of Darfur,
> I wish to inform you that the boundaries will be the same
> as they were before, and the limits will be from Om Shanga

to Tawaisha, Dar-el-Maalia, and Dar-el-Rizeigat as far as
the Bahr-el-Arab; then to Kalaka-el-Mullam, Dar-el-Taaisha
and the former boundary with Borgu [i.e., Waddai] (NA/
WO/106/14).[50]

Cartographic evidence from this period is much clearer than official
correspondence. The Anglo-Egyptian government claimed as its territory
all the land to the south of the Umbelacha River, which runs into the
Bahr al-Arab/Kiir River. This includes Hofrat al-Nahas, a settlement just
south of the Umbelacha. West of Hofrat al-Nahas, the border ran north
of the river, in a straight line to the Nile–Congo divide. Cartographic
evidence from this era is rich: learned societies in Europe were still
fascinated by the search for the sources of the Nile. Many of these maps
and papers were presented in the Government of Sudan's Memorial to
the Permanent Court of Arbitration (PCA) in the Hague in 2008, for a
tribunal that established the borders of Abyei, another enclave whose
borders must be delineated under the CPA.

The Government's Memorial makes clear that Hofrat al-Nahas was
part of Bahr al-Ghazal throughout the colonial period: the border in the
far west ran along the western source of the Nile or even to the north
of it. But during this period, there was a change to the idea of the Bahr
al-Arab/Kiir River as the border, albeit in an area to the east of the
area under study. In 1912, the British sponsored an agreement between
Rizeigat and Dinka Malwal people, which set the river as a tribal border.
The British overthrew Ali Dinar and incorporated Darfur into the Anglo-
Egyptian Sudan in 1916, as part of their calculations linked to the First
World War (the Kafia Kingi enclave became a hide-out for Ali Dinar's
defeated soldiers, as it had been for defeated Mahdists). The southern
border of Darfur once again became a provincial border, which in some
respects made its delimitation less urgent and allowed for pragmatic
approaches to border problems. One example of pragmatism was the
Munro–Wheatley agreement of 1924, which gave Rizeigat groups hunting

....

[50] Theobald (1965, p. 43) gives the date as 1901.

and grazing rights on a strip running 14 miles to the south of the Bahr al-Arab/Kiir River. The area had been emptied of population at the height of the slave trade but Dinka Malwal people returned there during the Mahdiya (Johnson, 2010). The British agreement to recognize Rizeigat grazing rights may have been a reward for military services: the British had used Rizeigat soldiers as a tribal militia during their campaign to overthrow Ali Dinar. The agreement eventually marked administrative boundaries in Northern Bahr al-Ghazal; in the Western district, it formed the basis for secondary rights.

5. The Arabs have general permission to enter the Western District Bahr El Ghazal Province to water and graze their cattle, between the river SOPO on the East and the river SHELEIKA on the West, and North of a line approximately twenty miles South of the river UMBELACHA.

6. The Arabs have permission to enter the Western District Bahr El Ghazal to hunt, provided they keep to the West of a line drawn from Sahafa on the Bahr El Arab to the junction of the rivers SOPO and BORO, and are in possession of a permit in English from the Nazir of their tribe. They must also obtain permission from the local chief in whose country they wish to hunt (DR.P/66-B-45).

Southern Policy and the transition to independence, 1930–55

This border flux of pragmatism and violence was abruptly replaced in the mid-1920s by closed districts and pass systems, which culminated in the creation of a no man's land in the north of Raga county as part of the ferocious version of the Southern Policy adopted by Brock (see Chapter 5) (B.G.P. 16.B.2). Subsequent measures limited the entry of northerners to the south: the former inhabitants of Kafia Kingi were not officially allowed to return, even if they had family on the other side of the border, but Habbaniya, Fellata and Rizeigat cattle-keepers had access. The 'Brock Line', running west-north-west from Kafia Kingi town, was established in 1931 as the grazing limit for Baggara groups crossing into the district (DP.R SCR 66-B-44).

The British were unable to police the boundary, and instead reviewed it at regular meetings between the two provinces, which were usually held at the border town of Safaha, to the east, in what is now Northern Bahr al-Ghazal state. They considered, and postponed decisions on proposals to:

- (1934) move the boundary southwards to 9°45', the latitude of Hofrat al-Nahas, bringing most of the south bank of the river into Darfur;

- (1934) build a road to Darfur so the Binga and Kara people could return to the enclave;

- (1939) repopulate the area with Awlad Arab, Mandala, or Kresh, because the lack of cultivation meant that the tsetse area was increasing, with economic consequences for cattle-keepers in Darfur;

- (1950s) repopulate the area with Awlad Arab, keeping it as part of Bahr al-Ghazal, but 'run[ning] it largely in Darfur's grazing interests' (SAD/815/7/12).

In 1941, the Munro–Wheatley agreement was amended, extending grazing rights by one day's travel south of the Brock Line at the start of the rains. The Brock Line also became the hunting boundary for the area to the east of Kafia Kingi (westwards, hunters could go to the FEA boundary) (SAD/815/7/10–11). The British began to relax restrictions on groups with links to Kafia Kingi wanting to move back there from the Umbelacha River. In 1951, Binga chief Mbanga Sheme wrote to British officials asking if the Binga people in Darfur could be allowed to resettle Kafia Kingi, complaining of oppressive taxation from the Habbaniya chief. British officials threatened to burn out any spontaneous returnees from Kafia

Kingi, but said that they would discuss the matter at the annual inter-province meeting.[51]

Administration of this border still required regular local negotiation over access rights, partly because it was too remote to police. But there was no change to the administrative border running along the Umbelacha in the British period. This only happened in 1960, when a presidential decree moved the boundary so that it ran down the Rikki River, creating the Kafia Kingi enclave.

Transfer of the Kafia Kingi enclave to the north, and the promise to return it, 1960–89

At this point the documentary record available for this study changes from being too copious to summarize to being almost non-existent. The decision to transfer the Kafia Kingi enclave to Darfur was taken by a military government under President Ibrahim Abboud. The government took power in 1958 partly in order to pre-empt a move to federalize Sudan, which would have given autonomy to Southern Sudan, then drifting towards war. People in Raga privately opposed the change to the boundary, but opportunities for protest were limited under the new authoritarian regime.[52] The reasons for the change may have been administrative: British personnel in Bahr al-Ghazal had frequently considered transferring to Darfur the town of Kafia Kingi or its surrounding area because of the cost of administering the remote region. British personnel in Darfur generally refused the offer, but Charles Julu, the governor of Western Bahr al-Ghazal, gave a speech at a 1985 border meeting stating that the 1960 change was an administrative response to the region's

....

[51] Letter from Sultan Mbange Sheme to D.C. Mr. R.C.S. MacPhail, Menamba, 12th May 1951, attached to WD/66-A-20/24 (RAGA).

[52] Interview with Muhammad Wadatallah, parliamentarian and Bahr al-Ghazal state commissioner on the Border Commission, April 2010.

remoteness.[53] Other depopulated border areas—such as Timsah and Ere, ancestral home of the Kaligi-speaking Feroghe group that lie near the border, due east of the enclave—were not transferred to Darfur.

Twelve years after the Abboud regime's decision to transfer the Kafia Kingi enclave to Darfur, a new Khartoum government committed itself to a return to the 1956 borders, a commitment requiring the return of the enclave to Bahr al-Ghazal. That promise was to be repeated several times over the next four decades, but in practice no change was ever made (see Figure 5).

The first civil war between Southern Sudan and the Khartoum government began between 1955 and 1962, and lasted through Abboud's military regime (1958–64) and the parliamentary period (1964–69) that followed. The war ended in 1972 with the Addis Ababa peace agreement between the rebels and the new military regime of President Gaafar Nimeiri (1969–83). The Addis agreement was the first of three peace agreements between the Sudanese government and armed groups linked to rebellions in Southern Sudan requiring a return to the 1956 borders (GoS et al., 1972, Article 3.iii). Raga and Wau people called for the enclave's return in a 1974 note to a government committee on internal borders (Committee For the Redivision of the Southern Provinces, nd, section 2, p. 38).

The implementation mechanisms for the Addis agreement were not as carefully scheduled as those of the CPA and no legislative measure was taken to return the Kafia Kingi enclave until a political crisis in 1980. A Regional Government bill for *northern* Sudan reached the National Assembly, to which was appended a map delineating five new regions in the north. According to one contemporary report:

> [The map] indicated obvious and even deliberate
> encroachments upon territories that were ostensibly part
> of the Southern Region. The areas affected were Kafia Kingi

---

[53] 'Speech of Lt Col Charles Julu Kyopo, secretary of the Sudan Socialist Union and Commissioner of the province of Western Bahr al-Ghazal, at the Safaha conference, 15 Jan 1985'. Unclassified photocopy provided by the Steering Committee of Kafia Kingi, Khartoum, April 2010.

FIGURE 5.
POST-INDEPENDENCE GOVERNMENTS AND BORDER DECISIONS

Date	Government	Wars and borders
1956–58	Parliamentary regime, Prime Ministers Ismail al-Azhari and Abdalla Khalil	Inconclusive discussions about southern federalism, no change to 1956 border
1956–64	Military government, President Ibrahim Abboud	(1960) Kafia Kingi enclave moved from Bahr al-Ghazal to Darfur; (1963) Anyanya rebellion in south, begins operations in Raga county; (1964) Anyanya Bahr al-Ghazal command established, attacks Wau
1964	Professionals Front, Prime Minister Sir al-Khatim al-Khalifa	Inconclusive attempts to end Anyanya rebellion
1964–69	Second parliamentary period, Prime Ministers M.A. Mahgoub and Sadig al-Mahdi	Intensification of war in south after failure of peace talks; beginnings of abolition of Native Administration
1969–85	Military government, President Gaafar Nimeiri (Sudan Socialist Union)	(1972) Addis Ababa agreement between government and Anyanya with commitment to return to 1956 borders between north and south; (1973) Southern Regional Government; 1970s abolition of Native Administration; (1979 or 1980 or 1982) Radom National Park established as a UNESCO Biosphere reserve; (1980–81) provincial reorganization fails to return Kafia Kingi to south; (1983) Regional Government dissolved, SPLM begins new rebellion in south

cont'd overleaf

1985–86	Transitional military government, President Suwar al-Dahab	(1985) Prime Minister Dafalla offers to rehabilitate the 1972 Addis Ababa agreement, which recognizes 1956 border; (1985) first SPLA attack on Raga
1986–89	Third parliamentary period, Prime Minister Sadig al-Mahdi	Intensification of war in south; partial restoration of Native Administration; (1986–87) SPLA attacks on Raga
1989–2004	*Ingaz* or National Salvation Revolution, President Omar al-Bashir; from 1997 led by the new National Congress Party (NCP)	Intensification of war in south; explicit Islamization of war; (1991) SPLA attempt to invade Darfur through Raga; (1991–94) reorganization of Native Administration and of provinces/states; (1995) reserved area of Radom National Park extended; (1997) Khartoum Peace Agreement with commitment to return to 1956 borders; (2001) SPLA capture Raga for duration of rainy season; (2003) war in Darfur; (2004) CPA Protocol on Power Sharing with commitment to return to 1956 borders
2005–present	NCP–SPLM Government of National Unity	(2005) Ceasefire in south; technical committee for border demarcation established; (2006) technical committee begins work

Source: author.

and the copper-rich Hofrat El Nahas areas in Bahr El Ghazal,
Bentiu, where oil production was planned, and the disputed
ethnically and culturally mixed border area of Renk in Upper
Nile Province (Badal, 1986, p. 144).

The Council of Ministers passed the bill to the Assembly without seeing
the appended map, and southern politicians protested that it constituted a violation of the Addis Ababa peace agreement. In response, the
president signed a decree on 31 December 1980 acknowledging that the
borders between the Southern Region and the north should remain as
they were at independence in 1956 (Badal, 1986, p. 146–51).

President Nimeiri had introduced the bill in response to a political
crisis discussed in Chapter 9 below—reshuffling internal borders was
intended to help him reshuffle alliances. But in reality he did not want his
decree ordering the return of the enclave to the south to be implemented.
Habbaniya groups petitioned him to keep the Kafia Kingi enclave in
Darfur as they used it for hunting—reportedly they told the president
that 'we will sell our cows and buy arms and protect it'.[54] Nimeiri gave
Ahmed Diraige, the newly-appointed governor of Darfur, the task of
stalling the implementation of the presidential decree.[55] In the south,
the Higher Executive Council (HEC, the semi-autonomous regional
government) established a committee under a former governor of Bahr
al-Ghazal, Isaiah Kulang, to oversee the enclave's handover in early 1981.
Protests in several Darfur towns erupted as the HEC committee arrived
in Nyala, where court buildings were set on fire. The committee arrived,
left immediately, and the handover was indefinitely postponed.[56]

Between 1979 and 1983 part of the Kafia Kingi enclave was declared
a national park and recognized by UNESCO as a Biosphere Reserve

....

[54] Interview with Ahmed Diraige, governor of Darfur 1980–83, October 2009.

[55] Interview with Ahmed Diraige, governor of Darfur 1980–83, October 2009.

[56] Interview with Ali Tamim Fartak, presidential adviser, former federal minister and
former governor of Bahr al-Ghazal; member in 1981 of the HEC committee, May 2010.

(different dates and areas of reservation are given by different sources).[57] Mining companies returned to Hofrat al-Nahas about this time too.[58] It is not clear why the government decided on a policy that underlined the enclave's remoteness and isolation just as it was being contested. 'At the time I never had it in mind that this was about the border,' said Yusuf Takana, then the minister of agriculture for Southern Darfur province, who was involved in decisions about the appointment of game police.[59]

In spite of disagreements about the return of Kafia Kingi to the south, annual meetings between Bahr al-Ghazal and Darfur officials at the border town of Safaha continued. These had been instituted in British times and they continued during the first civil war until the early 1980s.[60] They were usually held in February or March:

> The discussion would cover organization of pastures, resolution of disputes and tribal fights, collision between tribes in pastures, establishing good relations between tribal leaders, whether there is a problem. They meet for five days, slaughter rams, eat together, dance. All tribal leaders and administrators including the governor, who at that time was called commissioner.[61]

These meetings ended shortly after the war that followed the SPLM/A's 1983 rebellion against the Nimeiri government in Khartoum, after Nimeiri abrogated the Addis Ababa peace deal. The rebellion and a linked economic crisis soon led to the downfall of Nimeiri's regime, but the question of the Kafia Kingi enclave and the wider border did not receive

....

[57]   UNESCO (2007) gives the date as 1979; Yusuf Takana, then minister of agriculture for South Darfur province, gives the date as 1982, interview, 5 May 2010. See also extracts of a report in Arabic on the drugs trade in Radom Biosphere Reserve, see footnote 4.

[58]   Interview with retired miner, April 2010.

[59]   Interview with Yusuf Takana, former federal minister of international cooperation and former Darfur commissioner, Khartoum, May 2010.

[60]   Interview with Njagulgule chief Muhammad Ahmed Madibbo, Raga, March 2010.

[61]   Interview with Ali Tamim Fartak, Presidential adviser, former federal minister and former governor of Bahr al-Ghazal, May 2010.

much attention from the transitional regime and the parliamentary regime that replaced it.

Developments since 1989

The parliamentary regime lasted four years, until it was overthrown in a 1989 military coup led by current president Omar al-Bashir. One aim of the coup was to intensify the war against the southern rebels. Discussion of the north–south border and the Kafia Kingi enclave was excluded by war. In 1995, the Bashir government extended the reserved area of the Radom National Park to its current extent, of about 12,500 km2, displacing the population of its westernmost villages. Hunting, fishing and the use of agricultural equipment and even flour mills was banned, further isolating and depopulating the area.[62]

In the mid-1990s, the government became more involved in peace negotiations with southern armed groups. Several groups with origins in the SPLM rebellion had been become government allies, and in 1997 the government concluded the Khartoum Peace Agreement (KPA) with them. The KPA created the Coordinating Council of Southern States within the 1956 borders—which would require the return of the enclave to Bahr al-Ghazal. The 2005 CPA also acknowledged the 1956 borders as the borders of the autonomous southern region, and established a technical commission for border demarcation (GoS et al., 1997, Chapter 1; GoS and SPLM, 2005, Protocol on Power Sharing, Article 3.5).

The 1980 decree returning the enclave to Southern Sudan caused protests in Darfur. In 2010, the governor of South Darfur, Abd al-Hamid Musa Kasha made several statements pressing the case for Darfurian ownership of Hofrat al-Nahas.[63] By late 2010, the two parties to the CPA had failed to agree on the border, and governor Kasha's statements may be

....

[62]   Interviews with residents of the Kafia Kingi enclave, March 2010; interviews with members of the Steering Committee of Kafia Kingi, a Khartoum-based group of citizens of the area seeking its return to Southern Sudan, April–May 2010.

[63]   Sudan Radio Service (2010); Abd al-Azim (2010).

an indication that the ownership of Kafia Kingi was still in contention.

Before the Anglo-Egyptian era, there was no clear delineation of the southern border of Darfur, whose sphere of influence probably ended not very far south of the Umbelacha River and Bahr al-Arab/Kiir River. In the twentieth century, the Darfur sultanate claimed that Hofrat al-Nahas belonged to Darfur, but the sultan's intention to fly Condominium flags there probably means that he viewed it as a border station—the sultan's claim may imply that he recognized the rest of the enclave as another sphere. The British rejected the sultan's claim to Hofrat al-Nahas and by extension any claim to the rest of the enclave. The Anglo-Egyptian regime was the first to delineate the border in Bahr al-Ghazal: the line ran along the Umbelacha and Bahr al-Arab/Kiir River. A 1930 decision to create a cultural boundary along the political border complicated the situation, creating an enclave around Kafia Kingi that was empty of people, rich in minerals and easily tradeable. It was transferred to Darfur in 1960, probably for administrative reasons. But subsequent governments in Khartoum have all signed peace agreements requiring its return to the south, and in its submission to the PCA in The Hague, the present government implicitly acknowledged this.

7.   Border economies and the social meaning of roads, 1930–2010

The 1930–46 Southern Policy provoked some British administrators to write threatening letters to merchants in Raga town about Arab-style male dress. Such preoccupation with the organization of cultural symbols obscured the bigger historical shift that was taking place at the time. The extension of state reach brought about by roads and motorized vehicles, which drew formerly swiddening populations into tax systems and into markets for labour and grain, not always to their advantage. Road building was a key part of this process: people in the far west of Bahr al-Ghazal who had lived in river valleys were brought to villages along a road built largely by their own labour. Local chiefs were able to facilitate the provision of new services such as modern education, but they also became gang masters for construction labour and tax collectors for the newly settled population. In a subsistence society, poll taxes created a need for cash. Forced or tax labour was one way to pay off the poll tax; labour migration within Bahr al-Ghazal and beyond was another response to the cash demands that roads brought. Migration changed relationships within families and helped to spread small language groups across Sudan.

The roads from Raga had wide social meanings: the migrations that started on them tell a different story from the isolating cultural project of the Southern Policy. Roads also had economic meaning, but these were undermined by the Southern Policy's creation of cultural barriers, which held back the development of commercial relationships. The policy was an example of the contradictions of colonialism, whose principal aim was to increase or control the productivity of peripheral areas by bringing global market pressures to bear on every corner of Sudan. But political considerations—the need to prevent the development of national feeling by promoting local political communities and cultures—sometimes trumped economic development.

The roads from Raga were built after 1930 during a lull in the many wars that have been waged in Bahr al-Ghazal since the 1850s. Their military use may not have been readily apparent at the time of their construction but became evident when the lull ended, around the time of Sudan's independence in 1956. Although the roads were built after the violent pacification of Southern Sudan was completed, their construction was nonetheless a coercive process: state violence was at the centre of the economic development of Western Bahr al-Ghazal, which followed the building of the roads. Settling displaced populations along these roads, disciplining them as a labour force, and integrating them into a cash economy all required state violence to succeed.

Economic development, social change and state coercion were interconnected processes that helped the central Sudanese state shape its periphery. This chapter seeks to illustrate those interconnections by looking at roads in Raga county. This aspect of Raga's history provides a comparison for analyzing the construction and neglect of roads in Darfur, which helped make Darfur a separate peripheral region of the same state centre.

A new kind of economy in Bahr al-Ghazal

In 1930, before it was burnt to the ground by a British assistant district commissioner, Kafia Kingi town had a small market with 24 traders from northern Sudan (CS/16-B.1/4, p. 20). A track connecting it to Radom in South Darfur was the main trade route north, carrying modest exports (beeswax, chillies, sesame oil) to northern markets. Closure of the Kafia Kingi town and its market meant the abandonment of plans for a road linking Raga to Darfur, an economic loss to a government that partially justified the closure on the basis of financial considerations (B.G.P. 16.B.2). It was more than a loss of tax revenue: Kafia Kingi had a population that spread market disciplines and demand in an area where money was little used, and prices were controlled by chiefs and commissioners. People were being pushed towards *market* labour because they needed cash to pay the district's taxes, which were amongst the highest in Sudan at the time (SAD/710/65). In 1939, annual taxes in Raga were 20 piastres, and in Radom they were five: many people in Raga were sent to prison where they could work for one piastre a day to pay them off (unskilled labour outside prison was worth 1½ piastres a day) (No. 66 A 20/21). One governor of Darfur attributed the refusal of Kara and Binga people to leave Darfur to the labour system of the south, which had more in common with French and Belgian forced labour than the poll taxes of Darfur:

> [Binga people] were, before the [Kafia Kingi] reorganization,
> wild and difficult to administer and very averse to being
> settled on roads. Their refusal to return is, I think, due rather
> to their dislike of the system of taxed labour current in the
> Bahr el Ghazal and not in Darfur, than to Southern Policy,
> intermarriage with the Taaisha, and their attachment to their
> traditional homes (B.G.P./SCR/8-A-3).

Southern Policy in Western district (the present day Western Bahr al-Ghazal State) was implemented by settling the entire population of the district along a road from Wau to Boro Medina, a town near the border with FEA. The roads around Raga existed before the British arrived— Zubeir Pasha used one of them in his invasion of Darfur. But until the 1930s, they were tracks: porters provided the transportation services for many state projects. In 1939, the British planned to liquidate the colony of porters outside Wau who had provided these services (SAD/710/22).

The aim of the road from Wau to Boro Medina was administrative and cultural rather than economic. It did not improve access to markets, even though the British neo-primordialist approach needed cash to work. The British ended up generating this cash through forced road labour in the village, and aimed to suppress labour migration (migrants were called 'runaways') in order to maintain 'self-contained racial or tribal units' (Beshir, 1968, p. 115). These contradictions ensured the policy was short-lived, even though it created new demands for labour and a few bush shops in two decades of authoritarian peace. Roads were maintained by local people, under the chief's direction, and nearly all the road was populated: something of an achievement in a region that had suffered so much from deliberate depopulation.

By 1946, restrictions on travel north had been lifted and trade increased. After independence, the cash economy began to take off. A daughter of the Aja chief married with a bridewealth of just three piastres in 1959: other elements of the bridewealth such as hoes and labour donations were still more important then.[64] But in the 1960s, Raga began to export sorghum, sesame, groundnuts and cassava on the road running east to Aweil, a largely Dinka town in the flood plain. (In the 1940s, the government and the missionaries in Raga had to import grain from Aweil.)[65] Marriage became more monetized—by the late 1960s, a Raga merchant paid SDP 100 for a bridewealth.[66] The expansion of roads, villages and small towns were changing the face of society.

Independence and new wars in the south

Until 1960, the main route from northern Sudan to Wau was one that dated back to the days of the Khartoum slave trade: it involved a steamer to the White Nile port of Mashra al-Rekk, then overland to Wau. In 1960, the newly independent Republic of Sudan built railways to Wau and Nyala, connecting South Darfur and Western Bahr al-Ghazal to Khartoum's infrastructure. Raga's road links to the railhead at Wau may have become more economically important.[67] But within a few years, a civil war in the south had begun, linked to the problems of incorporating

....

[64]   Interview with El Nur Fadul, Aja chief, Raga, March 2010.

[65]   Interview with Arkangelo Musa Albino, NCP president and former commissioner of Raga county 2000–05, Raga, March 2010; SAD/529/1/5.

[66]   Interview with Tahir Juma, deputy NCP president, Western Bahr al-Ghazal, March 2010.

[67]   Interview with Ali Tamim Fartak, presidential adviser, former federal minister and former governor of Bahr al-Ghazal, Khartoum, April 2010; Interview with Camillo Kamin Sharf al-Din, former Anyanya commander, Raga, March 2010.

Sudan's most underdeveloped and diverse periphery into a centralized state. The war reached Raga county around 1963, and is discussed further in the next chapter.

During the wars of the nineteenth century and violent displacements of the 1930s, people would sometimes choose to retreat to the forest, the headwaters of a seasonal river, or even cross the watershed from or into the Nile basin. But the road seems to have changed things: in the wars of the 1960s, only a few people fled to the forest or over the watershed to the Central African Republic, which attained independence in 1960. Most used the roads to flee to towns—or the army forced them to move to towns, in order to deprive the rebels of popular support.[68] Like the Southern Policy for the British, the civil war was extremely effective for helping the Sudanese state attain its goals for the population of Raga county. Southern Policy had moved everyone to the road: the Sudanese Army countered the rebellion by moving everyone to the town. Interviewees described the process not as *nuzuh* (displacement, a word which also connotes wandering) but as *tahjir*, the forced migration of groups (the same word describing the Mahdist policy of moving whole tribes to the national capital). In a country with more than one word for war displacement, the choice of the word stressing the agency of the state is important.

The traumatic urbanization caused by the war that began in the early 1960s had wide cultural effects. In interviews in 2010, it was one of the most remembered social changes for Raga people. The war brought people from many different language groups with traditions of intermarriage to Raga. The use of Arabic as a domestic lingua franca became more widespread, and some languages began to die.

The road that had been populated almost all the way from Boro Medina to Wau was now empty, and most residents did not return when peace came in 1972. Yulu people, from a village called Deim Jallab, west of Raga, fled their village in 1965 and about 800 people returned after 2002, at

....

[68]   Interview with Arkangelo Musa Albino, NCP president and former Commissioner of Raga county, 2000–05, Raga, March 2010.

the behest of their chief, Hasan Ngere Sibian. Preservation of the Yulu language was a motivation for the return, and Yulu singing groups still sing songs about their return at celebrations. Aja people fled to Raga from Kparakpara, about 20 miles to the west of the town, and they never returned.[69]

After the 1972 peace deal: a new road north of Raga

The 1972 Addis Ababa Agreement gave Southern Sudan almost a decade of peace. In Raga, some people tried to reverse the displacements of the 1930s, which brought about the development of some new roads north. In the nineteenth century, many Feroghe and Bahr al-Ghazal Rizeigat groups had lived south of the border with Darfur, including in the areas around the settlement of Timsah beside two mountains, Jebel Ere and Tembeli. After the Mahdiya, they gradually moved southwards to Raga; but in the late 1960s, some decided to go back to their old area, where farming was good (Santandrea, 1964, p. 145). Timsah is nearer to South Darfur towns like El Daein than it is to Wau, and the links made by Feroghe and Bahr al-Gazal Rizeigat returning there helped orient Raga county towards northern markets and peoples.

The road from Raga to Timsah was the same road that Zubeir Pasha had used to invade Darfur in 1874. It had fallen into disuse in the twentieth century, and in the first civil war the Khartoum government army was more likely to use the old Kafia Kingi road, which was the long lorry route north until the 1980s.[70] The impetus for building a new road to Timsah came from a new war—the SPLM rebellion, which started in 1983. In 1984, the SPLA blew up the rail bridge over the Lol river, on the line connecting Wau with the north. Although the bridge was repaired,

....

[69] Interview with Hassan Ngere Sibian, Yulu chief, Raga, 4 March 2010; translation of Yulu song performed by Yulu singing group on the occasion of the visit of the president of the republic to Raga, 15 March 2010; interview with El Nur Fadul, Aja chief, Raga, 7 March 2010.

[70] Interview with people on the Raga–Boro Medina road that once led to Kafia Kingi, March 2010.

and the railway line held (using exceptionally brutal counter-insurgency tactics), the attack had demonstrated Wau's vulnerability to the southern rebels.[71] Ali Tamim, then governor of Bahr al-Ghazal and a member of the Feroghe leading family (on the government's side), supported efforts to improve the road from Raga to Timsah. According to some intervie-wees, certain figures in the central government opposed the upgrading of Zubeir's road, which had once wrought such dramatic transformations on Sudanese history.[72]

But Raga groups, with the support of Feroghe notables and govern-ment officials such as Ali Tamim, were able to build the road themselves. Al-Tom al-Nur, a private contractor and official of the Sudan Socialist Union (SSU), was also involved. His father was Ndogo, a small Fertit group living to the west of Raga town, and had travelled to Kordofan and married his mother, from the Misseriya group of Baggara pastoralists there. In 1984, al-Tom al-Nur, now a Khartoum-based political opponent of the SPLA and major general in the SAF, was setting up the Peace Forces, a pro-Khartoum militia force that held Raga county and its roads for the government for almost the entire duration of the subsequent war. With the backing of Ali Tamim, al-Tom al-Nur persuaded Indiri, Feroghe and Shatt chiefs to provide him with free labour. Workers from these tribes took part in a project that may have reminded older people of British labour mobilization. No mechanical implements were used and the road remains a rough one—it takes a lorry more than a day to get from Raga to Timsah, a distance of 90 miles.

Roads during the 1983–2005 civil war and after the CPA

The Timsah road was subsequently extended up to El Daein, a town in

---

[71] Interview with Mark Nyipuoc, SPLA lieutenant-general and governor of Western Bahr al-Ghazal state from 2006–09, March 2010; interview with Ali Tamim Fartak, presidential adviser, former federal minister and former governor of Bahr al-Ghazal, Khartoum, April 2010.

[72] Interview, name and place withheld, March 2010.

South Darfur associated with the leading family of the Rizeigat Baggara group, and it became the main supply route for the government in western areas of the war-torn south. Al-Tom al-Nur's Peace Forces militia was financed by protection levies on the convoys of lorries driven by Darfurian and Kordofanian men that formed at Raga to travel to Wau—50 or even 100 at a time. The road was expanded as traffic increased and the market in Raga town was upgraded.[73] Lorries supplied garrisons and towns and sometimes took loads of cassava, sweet potato, sesame, groundnuts, teak and mahogany back to the north.[74] The road was called 'the lifeline' because of its strategic importance to the government's war in Bahr al-Ghazal and the market access it provided. The Peace Forces held the road for almost the entire duration of the war. Al-Tom al-Nur recalls certain opposition to the road as it crossed the cultural and ecological borderlines in Raga county, but also the possibilities it brought:

> Lawrence Wol Wol was the governor of Wau. He wrote an
> angry letter because I was bringing Islam to Wau. But six
> months later there was a famine in Wau, 80 lorries arrived.[75]

When wars aligned local interests with those of central government groups in the periphery were able to undertake self-resourced initiatives such as the Raga–Timsah road. War brought wealth along the road: the development tax on goods, levied on lorry cargoes, became the main source of revenue for local government.[76] During wartime, Raga enjoyed a boom: a small town on a vital supply route, it could have 50 lorries parked in its market at any one time. But peace brought an end to this economic growth and today just ten lorries in the market square would

....

[73] Interview with Abd al-Hamid Hassan Gayli, chair of Raga Chamber of Commerce 2007–10, March 2010.

[74] Interview with al-Tom al-Nur, SAF major general and leader of the Peace Forces militia, 1984–2006, May 2010.

[75] Interview with al-Tom al-Nur, SAF major general and leader of the Peace Forces militia, 1984–2006, May 2010.

[76] Interview with Joseph Valentino, director of taxation, Raga county, March 2010.

seem a large number.[77] The sensitive road north, once the lifeline of the SAF, is now a military zone, closed to foreigners and punctuated with checkpoints and barracks. Lorries going north usually travel empty because Bahr al-Ghazal's trade with the north is now routed through the roads and railways of Kordofan.

The Raga–Timsah road illustrates the way in which development and conflict are entangled in Sudan. The 1983–2005 civil war saw the upgrading of a number of tracks and other roads as populations moved around. In the late 1980s, people from Darfur began migrating to the under-populated areas to the east of the Kafia Kingi enclave. Firga and Sere Malaga, once tiny Yulu settlements lying in this region, were resettled by Fertit people.[78] Baggara farmers from the Habbaniya and Rizeigat tribes moved to the land and water around Timsah to grow sorghum for export to Darfur (though some stayed only for sowing and harvesting, spending the rest of the time back in Darfur).[79] South Darfur state authorities in Radom provided a small amount of investment in these areas, perhaps as part of a plan to extend Darfurian control of the region. The Sudanese Red Crescent Society financed the upgrading of a road from Timsah to Firga around 2000. It was another example of the close relationship between war and development—resources for road building came from humanitarian aid budgets that came to the area because of the conflict.

Rizig Zakaria was elected governor of Bahr al-Ghazal in 2010. He had fought in al-Tom al-Nur's pro-Khartoum government Peace Forces during the 1980s, and then defected to the SPLA, leading its successful attack on Raga in 2001, which displaced many Raga people to Darfur. When government forces recaptured the town some months later, Zakaria warned the population that the SAF would exact a heavy retribution, setting off the last major wave of displacement from Raga town. Many people fled to

....

[77] Interview with merchants in Raga market, Raga, March 2010.

[78] Interviews with Miskin Musa Abd al Mukarram, executive director, Timsah, Raga county, 20 March 2010; interview with Suleiman Hussein Abdullahi, Sara chief, Firga, 21 March 2010.

[79] Interview, name and place withheld, April 2010.

Tambura, in SPLA-controlled Western Equatoria, or to CAR. A handful of terrified fugitives from the battle fled to the forest, but few stayed there to follow the forest lifestyles of their ancestors. Most twenty-first century fugitives travelled to refugee camps—another example of the pervasive urbanization that the roads had wrought.

In 2004, Zakaria ordered SPLA forces to construct a road from Tambura to Deim Zubeir so that Fertit people who had been displaced to Tambura could go straight home. According to an SPLA officer who was in Tambura at the time, Zakaria wanted a direct route to Raga county to discourage people from returning via Wau, where they might be tempted to settle for an urban life. Other interviewees confirmed that, unlike other displaced persons, their return to Raga was not assisted by humanitarian air flights, which might have transited through urban centres.[80] The Tambura displaced were seen as an SPLM constituency for a sensitive border area, a counterweight to the groups that had taken the road to Darfur instead and might become a constituency for the NCP as a result. Roads were helping to solidify political differences amongst Fertit groups: between those who had gone to Darfur and those who had gone to Equatoria. For some of the displaced of 2001, their ethnicity had been a factor in their choice of destination.

Developing peripheries: roads and railways in South Darfur

The story of Raga's roads illustrates the way that Sudan's periphery has been developed. Economic and infrastructural growth have been inevitably entangled with warfare. It also illustrates the way in which the periphery is created: how a hinterland becomes defined by its relation to a new centre. South Darfur's roads and railway offers another illustration of peripheral development.

In the early 1960s, a new railway line to Nyala in South Darfur connected this hinterland to the centre. This led to a boom in cash crops in an

....

[80]   Interviews, names and places withheld, March 2010.

area where, previously, cultivation had been a low-status, subsistence niche. Farming was historically associated with slavery—a link quietly perpetuated by Anglo-Egyptian officials in Darfur in the name of social order. The slaves had mostly come from Bahr al-Ghazal and had been slowly incorporated into Baggara society (some manumission warrants were dated in the 1950s) (Hargey, 1999, pp. 254–61).[81] By contrast, from the 1960s, farming took on a new meaning as more productive farms provided an entry into the cash economy and into socially important networks (Adams, 1982, pp. 263ff). 'This is when slaves became masters,' says Yusuf Takana, an academic and former cabinet minister who is a member of a leading Buram family.[82]

While cash agriculture changed occupational hierarchies other developments were also transforming the region. A series of droughts from the late 1960s precipitated migration from North to South Darfur, especially amongst Zaghawa groups, whose livelihoods were based around camel-herding and cultivation. In 1973, the president issued a decree supporting the move of Zaghawa groups from drought-affected North Darfur to South Darfur. The moves were encouraged by some Zaghawa leaderships (de Waal, 1989, pp. 91ff).[83] Many of them moved to the goz soils of South Darfur, which had become much more suitable for cash agriculture with the introduction of boreholes (widely introduced in the modernization schemes of the 1970s) (de Waal, 1989, p. 102). The empty lands north of the Kafia Kingi enclave had acquired new value, and their population a new ethnic diversity.[84]

Increased land values and social diversity worked well for everyone at first, but eventually they contributed to land disputes that are implicated in the current civil war in Darfur, which began in 2003. Another

....

[81]   And interview with member of a leading Habbaniya family.

[82]   Interview with Yusuf Takana, former federal minister of international cooperation and former Darfur commissioner, Khartoum, May 2010.

[83]   Interview with Mohamed Ali, Nyala citizen.

[84]   Interview with Yusuf Takana, former federal minister of international cooperation and former Darfur commissioner, Khartoum, May 2010.

factor behind this civil war, discussed further in Chapter 10, is the lack of development in the area, which led to the emergence of Darfurian regionalist movements, such as the Darfur Development Front, as far back as the 1960s. In the 1970s, agricultural modernization plans aimed at addressing Darfur's economic underdevelopment, but African droughts and global economic crises in the 1970s and 1980s prevented these plans from becoming a reality, and Sudan drifted into a period of civil war and extended economic crisis.

The promise of development in the goz lands of South Darfur was undermined by the outbreak of war and the cutting off of investment. Some groups in the area sought new economic opportunities, which arose from war not from agricultural expansion. The crisis of the 1970s and 1980s contributed to the outbreak of the second civil war, when some Darfurian groups, including Rizeigat Baggara elements, joined a ferociously predatory war economy in the flood plains of the south. Deployed to protect the railway line to Wau, these militias created six miles of scorched earth on either side of it, strategically destroying the Dinka cattle economy and its social base.[85] Dinka people, particularly women and children, were abducted and used for forced labour in a practice echoing the nineteenth century slave trade (Jok, 2001, pp. 21ff). Raga was largely spared from this pillage economy, but Darfurians there could participate in a different war economy of convoys and hoarding. But neither convoys nor pillage in the south could hope to address Darfur's chronic underdevelopment. Sudan's slow recovery from the global financial crisis of the 1970s cut off investment to the peripheries for three decades (World Bank, 2003, p. 46).

The lack of a transport network in Darfur has prevented economic development. In 2009, the cost of transporting a Nyala sheep from Darfur to a ship in Port Sudan was half the sheep's market value (World Bank, 2009, p. 79). The *Ingaz* (National Salvation) government that came to power in a 1989 coup agreed to the construction of a Western Salvation

....

[85] Interview with Mark Nyipuoc, SPLA lieutenant-general and governor of Western Bahr al-Ghazal state from 2006–09, March 2010.

road that would connect Darfur with the infrastructure of the Nile valley. State governments of Darfur and Kordofan financed the road by selling their state quota of sugar, but for the past 13 years it has not progressed west of al-Nahud in Kordofan.[86] The sugar in this story encouraged some unsurprisingly bitter poetry:

> We, in the West, demand asphalt.
> We would swap sugar for asphalt.
> Sugar is not sweeter than asphalt.
> But we find neither sugar nor asphalt...
> Don't lie to us because lies look like asphalt.
> For two years you promised us asphalt,
> But ten years have gone and asphalt doesn't come yet.

(Translation of poem by Abdelhamid Abbas, quoted in Tubiana, 2009, pp. 195–218.)

Societies that were reshaped in the twentieth century in response to global economic forces required a parallel investment in roads in order to expand their local market economies and link them into the international system. Where there was a lack of such infrastructural development people were forced to seek alternatives means of income generation. Predation and migration were two common strategies in the 1990s, with the former often seen as more lucrative—as suggested by the Arabic phrase *nahab yawmayn wala ightirab sanatayn* (two days robbery is better than two years of migrant labour) (Ibrahim, 2008, p. 183).

Predation and migration are two ways to deal with such economic crises in the periphery. Drugs are another: by creating a trade in small quantities of high value goods, they allow people to circumvent the obstacles to market access that constrain most other livelihoods in this region. In the remote Kafia Kingi enclave, cut off from lorry traffic for half the year, drug cultivation is an important strategy. A 1994 study in South Darfur and Bahr al-Ghazal found that hashish cultivation began

....

[86] Interview with former government official, Khartoum, October 2009.

in the region in the 1940s among farmers from the Runga, Bornu and Tunjur tribes. The first farm was in al-Muraya village, north of Radom, in an area settled by Awlad Arab groups from Kafia Kingi. Traders from El Daein, Nyala and El Obeid arrived in the 1950s and hashish cultivation began to spread. Local processing improved, and some villages became associated with this one crop. Farm sizes varied from 0.4 to 6.3 hectares, and while crop yields for rice, chickpeas and sesame were high, limited access to markets for these conventional crops increased the popularity of growing hashish. The 1994 study found that hashish was cultivated on 182 farms covering nearly 100 hectares and producing an estimated 64,385 kg that year, valued at about SDP 26.1 billion, equivalent to USD 47 million at that time (Mohamed et al., 1998, pp. 114–21).

Another study was conducted in the late 1990s after the extension of the nature reserve in the Kafia Kingi enclave. This decision introduced legal restrictions on conventional agriculture and pushed people into honey gathering, hunting and drug cultivation. The study found that outside investors (most of them from Darfur) financed much of the drug cultivation.[87] Production is mainly for local markets and has become an important part of commerce in some South Darfur towns. One preacher interviewed stated: 'I spoke in the mosque of Abu Matarig about the dangers of drugs and they said, "Are you crazy? Everyone depends on the drugs trade." '[88]

Roads and peripheries of the future

Most of Sudan's asphalt roads are in the northern Nile valley, the economic heartland of the state. The CPA required a change in the relationship between this centre and the periphery. It established an autonomous

....

[87]   In extracts of a report in Arabic on the drug trade in Radom Biosphere Reserve that appears to have been commissioned by the South Darfur state ministry of agriculture and livestock in the late 1990s, provided by an NGO official who is also a member of the NCP in Radom.

[88]   Interview with mosque preacher, Khartoum, May 2010.

government in the poorest region, the south, and a commission for state-level ministries of finance—the Fiscal and Financial Allocations Monitoring Commission (FFAMC)—which would set the framework for the investment of Khartoum resources in the periphery (Thomas, 2009, p. 30). That commission was incorporated into subsequent peace agreements that were intended to bring to an end to other uprisings in Darfur and eastern Sudan (GoS and Eastern Front, 2006, Article 63; GoS et al., 2006, Articles 120–26). Investment rates in Darfur's transportation are still disappointing today, while the new autonomous government of Southern Sudan has invested considerable resources, outperforming northern Sudanese and British administrations in five short rollercoaster years.[89]

New GoSS roads have transformed Bahr al-Ghazal. The road from Raga to Aweil was upgraded in 2008, and a new gravelled road runs from Muglad in Kordofan to Wau town, linking Southern Sudan to the tarred road network concentrated in the centre of Sudan, in the northern Nile valley. The contractor for the Muglad road is now building a road with four steel bridges from Wau to Raga.[90] This all-season road has transformative potential: it will probably end the *takhzin* system, in which food is stockpiled at the end of the dry season and prices rise in towns cut off by river inundations, a system that turns the hunger gap before harvest into the highlight of the financial year. The road will draw Raga into the economy of the southern hinterland and away from that of Darfur and the Nile valley, where once it played an intermediary role.

In the past, roads in Bahr al-Ghazal were built in the shadow of coercive state projects or wars. The roads built in the complex and tense CPA period may still have a military rationale, but this time they are being built by firms rather than by coerced or unpaid labour of local people. GoSS has contracted an exceptionally competent company, Eyat Oilfield Services Co., to build the road. Established in 2004, with head offices in

---

[89] Investment in transport and roads made up 12.4 per cent of the 2008 Supplementary Budget in the south. Ministry of Finance and Economic Planning (2008, p. 5).

[90] See <http://www.eyatoil.com/RB/Projects.html#>

Khartoum, it has succeeded in Sudan's sticky oil services sector—GoSS sources complain of the links between this sector and the ruling party in Khartoum. Eyat's mission statement is phrased in optimistic language that is internationally recognizable:

> *'Our mission is to push forward the wheel of development in Sudan by relentlessly executing major infrastructure and development projects.'* Eyat Oilfield Services Co. Ltd. was established in 2004 for the sole purpose of developing the country in various fields, it's a 100% Sudanese owned company with the total number of 200 employees. I'm proud to say that Eyat now stands as the biggest company in Sudan 'and the second biggest in Africa' in terms of Machineries & Equipments. We pride ourselves on daring to push the boundaries of what's possible, in other words what has been accomplished by Eyat in the South of Sudan in terms of Roads & Bridges is nothing less than 'MIRACLES' And we will continue endeavouring to develop our great country in every possible way... now and forever (Elbashier, 2010).

GoSS chose Eyat, with its quaint globalese and Khartoum connections, to build very sensitive roads north: in 2008, its contracts with Eyat made up 49 per cent of total published transport and infrastructure contracts (Ministry of Finance and Economic Planning, 2008, p. 22). This is a vivid, if unexpectedly upbeat, predictor of future economic relationships between GoSS and well-connected northern firms. It is also a predictor of future labour relations: instead of coercing local workers, the government is paying for outsiders to come and build the south.

This optimism and sense of change contrasts with available evidence about the economic future of Darfur. 'Development of physical infrastructure that will improve Darfur states access to their main markets as well as to the rest of the Sudan and neighbouring countries' is one of the commitments in the 2006 Darfur Peace Agreement (DPA), which marked the end of hostilities between the government and one major rebel faction in Darfur, the Sudan Liberation Army (SLA) of Minni Minnawi, many of whose forces are drawn from the Zaghawa ethnic group (GoS et al., 2006, Article 147.6). Little development has been realized in the four years since it was signed. According to one Rizeigi interviewee, GoSS asked the tribal leadership for approval for a road from Safaha, the border town on the Bahr al-Arab/Kiir River, to El Daein, the home of the Rizeigat paramount chief. Rizeigat leaders agreed, but the Khartoum government said no:

> 'The Rizeigat youth said—now SPLA can get to the river in a crisis but you [the government] can't.'
>
> 'Why did the government refuse the El Daein road?'
>
> 'Because they didn't want the SPLM to have a presence in society.'[91]

---

[91] Interview with Rizeigi person, name and place withheld, May 2010.

8.   Bahr al-Ghazal and Darfur in Sudan's first civil war and peace deal

The civil war that was fought between Southern Sudan and the central government in the 1950s and 1960s took place in a region where ethnic affiliation had been the basis of externally-imposed political order for over a century. Raga people largely supported the war against the centre, and most of the population along the county's main road were forcibly displaced to towns. The war brought Raga people in contact with wider southern politics, but at the end of the war, previously unrecorded tensions emerged between the Fertit people of Raga and the Nilotic people of the flood plains.

It was the beginning of a turn to ethnic politics in Sudan's periphery. The main alternative to ethnic politics at the time was the vision of modern national development. Development schemes in the border-lands of South Darfur in the 1970s and 1980s promised a different kind of Sudan, but the schemes fell apart in a global economic crisis that hit the country hard. In Darfur and in Southern Sudan, the central government began to reconfigure the periphery around identity politics instead, setting the stage for a new outbreak of war. This chapter examines these developments, from 1955 to 1983.

Anyanya 1—Sudan's first post-independence civil war

In 1955, the British were preparing to leave Sudan, and British officers and commissioners in the south had been replaced by northern personnel. Across Equatoria, riots and mutinies accompanied the birth of the new order. After these short-lived uprisings were repressed, southern politicians took part in the new political institutions in Khartoum, supporting a parliamentary vote for Sudan's immediate independence (which came in 1956) and also pushing for federal arrangements for Southern Sudan. A military coup in 1958 ended this discussion, and led to a programme to incorporate the south into Khartoum's version of the nation. They aggravated the still-existing coercive policies of the colonial era—poll taxes, forced labour, lower wage scales for Southerners—with a tactless and eventually brutal programme of Arabization and Islamization that targeted educated Southerners for transfer out of the south, imprisonment, torture and assassination (Garang, 1971, p. 9; Reining, 1966, p. 34). 'It was all a blind, thoughtless reaction to the Southern Policy of the 1930s... which was long dead by 1947,' comments Abel Alier, then a southern judge working in the north (Alier, 2003, p. 40).

Raga people largely supported the rebels. In 1955, Camillo Kamin Sharf al-Din was a 23-year-old soldier from Deim Zubeir in the Equatorial Corps, the colonial government's army in the south. He was one of four Kresh soldiers who made up the small Fertit group there. After the mutiny, he fled to Kenya and then Uganda where in the early 1960s he encountered southern politicians like Saturnino Lohure and William Deng in Kampala who were seeking to recruit former Equatorial Corps soldiers (Fula Boki Tombe Gale, 2002, p. 233). The main southern movement was at the time called Sudan African National Union (SANU), and it set up an army, called Anyanya, in 1963 (Fula Boki Tombe Gale, 2002, pp. 235ff). Camillo decided to join the rebel movement: 'For our country. Those Arab people, they killed people, they took small children, they took our young people.' He went into Sudan to fight with other former soldiers, armed with a stick. They had to attack police posts to get weapons, and the different soldiers headed for their home areas. He and his Anyanya comrades in Bahr al-Ghazal—all Fertit or Zande soldiers—attacked the small convoys of lorries (about seven a month) on the road from Wau to Boro Medina, from camps in the bush. In response, the Sudanese army forced many people out of the villages on the road, where they had been neatly ordered by the British 1930 campaign of forced movement. By the mid-1960s, most of the people of the area were living in towns, not villages, and many of them did not return at the end of the war.

Muhammad Wadatalla retired as an MP in 2010 at the end of a political career spanning more than 50 years. He was born in Kafia Kingi in 1925 and in 1930 his family was forcibly moved to Lilli, east of Boro Medina, where Kresh Hofra people were rehoused. His father sent him to a school run by a northern religious teacher in Gossinga, the Njagulgule village east of Raga, from where he moved to Radom to study more Quran and grow chillies. He then went to Khartoum and received a scholarship to Al-Azhar, then a religious university and proponent of conservative, state-sanctioned versions of Sunni Islam. In 1958 he returned to Raga and stood for parliament representing a northern party, the Democratic Unionists. He lost to Stanislaus Peysama (a Darfurian standing for a southern party). By the early 1960s, however, he was involved in the rebellion.

> The government did not want southerners to be educated.
> [Former prime minister Muhammad Ahmad] Mahgoub did
> not want anyone in the south to know his ABC.[92]

Anyanya 1 imposed the traumatic urbanization that is part Sudanese warfare on the ordinary people from Raga county. In one of the most far-reaching social changes in the area thousands people moved from the road to the town—on most stretches of the road from Wau to Raga, the displacement of the 1960s has still not been reversed. Displacement to southern towns like Wau helped bring people into contact with movements that linked them to the wider south. SANU had Bahr al-Ghazal representatives at its 1964 National Convention, and Anyanya had a Bahr al-Ghazal command whose daring 1964 attack on Wau (led by Bernardino Mou) alerted Khartoum to the strength of the movement (Fula Boki Tombe Gale, 2002, p. 244; Alier, 2003, p. 40).

Anyanya and its linked southern political movements were dominated by people from Equatoria (the rebel army's name comes from the word for snake poison in an Equatorian language, Madi) (Fula Boki

....

[92]   Interview with Muhammad Wadatallah, parliamentarian and Bahr al-Ghazal state commissioner on the Border Commission, April 2010.

Tombe Gale, 2002, p. 31). Like the smaller population of Western Bahr al-Ghazal, Equatorian people were agrarian; amongst the first group to be 'pacified' by British security forces and amongst the first to be educated by missionaries. The Dinka and Nuer people of the flood plains emerged from colonial rule ill-equipped for participation in modern political and military structures, having resisted colonial rule and colonial education the longest (in part because of their inclinations to pastoralism, and because colonial education aimed to stratify their societies, which had many egalitarian tendencies). Colonial education systems had thus been dominated by Equatorians and people of Western Bahr al-Ghazal who went on to dominate the Anyanya rebellion. But all participants in Anyanya—Dinkas, Equatorians and the peoples of Western Bahr al-Ghazal—needed to use local connections to fight a rebellion where logistics and intelligence networks were non-existent. They had to fight from their 'self-contained tribal and racial units' (Beshir, 1968, p. 115) of the Southern Policy, that still imposed its neo-primordialist limitations on communications and logistics across the south.

Local militias and the consolidation of ethnic boundaries in the 1970s

Organizing a national movement around local militias contributed to tribal tensions in the south, which generated some colourfully named but forgotten institutions such as the Anyidi Revolutionary Government and the Sue River Republic, which aimed at promoting tribal or language-group interests (Badal, 1994, p. 107). These tensions emerged after the 1972 Addis Ababa peace agreement too. People from Nilotic societies, educated in exile, came back to look for jobs in the new government. Equatorians and people from Bahr al-Ghazal felt that too many of these jobs went to Nilotic people—Dinka and Nuer—even when a Regional Assembly in Juba with a Dinka majority elected an Equatorian to lead the HEC. For about two years from 1973, Raga lost its county headquarters to Aweil, a predominantly Dinka town, and was incorporated in a parliamentary constituency held by a Dinka politician; many

local administrators were Dinka and Nuer.[93] People of the area told a
visiting committee around this time:

> There is the intense feeling of the Fertit of Wau and Raga
> against the Dinka and there is the strong aspiration for a
> separate province for them. The Fertit, they said, are afraid of
> being dominated by the Dinka and insisted that they wanted
> to preserve their ethnic interests. They expressed strongly
> that they don't want to join a province with the Dinka...
> Failing a separate province they asked that these Councils
> should join with their neighbours to the south—the Azande
> (Committee For the Redivision of the Southern Provinces, nd,
> Section 2, p. 57).

In Western Bahr al-Ghazal, the use of ethnicity to create administrative boundaries had many precedents. In the 1980s, some Fertit leaders
promoted this idea. A secret paper of alleged Dinka provenance circu-
lated in Raga in the 1970s or 1980s, entitled 'Dinka Policy Against Fertit
Groups'. It reportedly stated that Dinka people were planning to marry
the daughters of Fertit people (for a man, Fertit marriage customs are
simpler and cheaper than Dinka ones), and it threatened that Dinka cows
would be tied up under Fertit mango trees (Raga county is famous for
its mangoes).[94]

The ethnic tensions between Fertit and Dinka people appear to have
emerged in the period following the 1972 Addis Ababa peace agreement.
A partial review of the historical records finds no references to Dinka–
Fertit antagonisms before then, despite the fact that both groups lived
through the brutal upheavals of the slave raiding period, when they
were, in some cases, pitted against each other as allies or victims of the
slavers. Indeed, there is some evidence of mutual support: Ndogo people
fled to Dinka areas from Zande raids in the late nineteenth century;

[93] Interview with Ali Tamim Fartak, presidential adviser, former federal minister and
former governor of Bahr al-Ghazal, Khartoum, April 2010.
[94] Interview with Fertit intellectual, name and location withheld, March 2010.

and as late as 1917, Shatt people took refuge from Rizeigat attacks in Dinka areas (SAD/815/7/34; Santandrea, 1964, p. 54). Until the 1970s, Dinka fishermen would migrate seasonally to the Sopo and Raga rivers to catch and sell fish: 'Our relations were good,' said one NCP official from Raga.[95]

Changes to administrative borders appear to have been the trigger for Fertit fears of engulfment by the much larger Dinka language group to the south—this and the sense that the success of the SPLA was turning this language group into an invincible political community. Across the south, boundary politics pitted ethnic groups against each other, even though boundary changes in the land-rich region made little change to everyday life (Nyaba, 2000, p. 26).

Alternatives to ethnic politics: development in Darfur, 1960s and 1970s

In the 1970s, ethnic consciousness was intensifying in Western Bahr al-Ghazal, making people more aware of boundaries between different groups. At the same time, Nimeiri's government was planning an alternative future for peripheral Sudan and its relations with the centre. The government hoped that the contradictions it had inherited from the colonial era could be reworked through 'modernization', which at the time meant development plans that could turn traditional societies into modern ones—that is, more monetized, more urbanized, more industrialized. This process was intended to create a unified national identity from the patchwork of colonial identities.

Agricultural schemes were set up across Sudan's hinterland. The Western Savannah Project (WSP) was established in South Darfur (Seekers of Truth and Justice, 2004, p. 23), covering the area of Goz Dango (also called the western goz, or al-Goz al-Gharbi), which runs to the north of the Umbelacha River. According to a 1974 survey for the

....

95 Interview with Arkangelo Musa Albino, NCP president and former commissioner of Raga county 2000–05, Raga, March 2010.

project, the population of Goz Dango was 58,094 at this time (Hunting Technical Services, 1974, p. 7). This included Kara and Binga people who had fled Kafia Kingi in 1930, as well as many others who were relatively recent drought migrants. The latter were mostly Zaghawa people, camel pastoralists of the semi-arid north who faced heavy pressures in the droughts of the 1970s and 1980s and responded with great ingenuity, developing new livelihoods in farming (in Goz Dango and adjacent areas of South Darfur) and trade.

> Seventy per cent of the population of al-Goz al-Gharbi were Zaghawa who moved there between 1973 and 1976 during drought and after fighting [in North Darfur] with Arab camel herders—Nimeiri issued a decree to move them in 1973, and the Habbaniya wanted them to come because it was a jungle, nobody was using the area. Elephants and lions, and a lot of flies too. Habbaniya are not good at farming or agriculture and they used their labour. Habbaniya owned the land and the Zaghawa were labour… In the 1980s because of the vast areas the Habbaniya would sell the land, and Zaghawa owned a lot of lands. They are hard working and come from north, they bred cattle, and owned trucks; they became the main suppliers for the area… In 1983 another drought led to displacement of Masalit, Tama, Erenga, Gimir, Masalati, Misseriya Jebel—they did not come officially and they were labour for the Zaghawa and Habbaniya… All tribes reported to Habbaniya nazir.[96]

The ingenuity and discipline of the drought migrants were an important component of their successful adaptation. Their crops contributed to increasing yields in Darfur in the 1970s, which helped the region manage a period of drought without famine (de Waal, 1989, p. 71). And investments such as those of the WSP made an important contribution.

....

[96] Interview with Mohamed Ali, Nyala citizen, Khartoum, April 2010.

But a global economic crisis brought the WSP and all other agricultural schemes outside the developed core of Sudan to an end in the 1980s.

The 1980s: the end of development and the return to rural conflict

The economic crisis of the 1970s marked an end to the long boom that followed the Second World War. Many of the costs of the crisis were passed to Third World economies, engulfing Sudan in the process. Like other countries, Sudan sought to buy time for modernization by running up huge short-term debts, not realizing that modernization itself had changed for good, and that its debts would soon expose all of Sudanese society to a global financial market that they could not hope to control.

The WSP ended in the 1980s, when the central government transferred responsibility for its administration to Darfurian authorities—passing the costs of its crisis to Sudan's periphery (Young et al., 2005, p. 20). The ending of this and all the other remote rural agricultural schemes was cited in the *Black Book* as an example of the way in which Sudan's periphery is created. The *Black Book* was distributed secretly in Khartoum in 2000 and is often attributed to the leadership of the Justice and Equality Movement (JEM), a Darfurian rebel movement established in 2003 with a Zaghawa leadership. According to this text:

> ... schemes were established within this [mechanized rain-fed agricultural] sector with the aim of developing deprived areas and rehabilitating drought stricken savannah belt. Rather than augment this sector, the government ordered liquidation of a number of them [the WSP is listed]... None of these schemes were in the north [the northern Nile valley, the economic core of the state] and that these schemes were liquidated and not sold or privatized. We add that these schemes were developmental and their contribution was not confined to economic gains. As such we are bound to conclude that scrapping of these schemes indicates that development

work is a preserve of north Sudan [the northern Nile valley]
(Seekers of Truth and Justice, 2004, p. 23).

The end of this experiment in peripheral economic development re-em-
phasized the economic dominance of the northern Nile valley, and marked
a return to the politics of ethnic conflict in rural Sudan. In Goz Dango,
conflict arose between Zaghawa and Habbaniya people, while Kara and
Binga people were drawn into separate but related violence. The *Black
Book*'s authors implicate this change in agricultural development policy
in the war in Darfur that began two decades later.

Reconfiguring the periphery: the backdrop to a long civil war

Nimeiri maintained power through a constant adjustment of alliances
and constitutional structures. Variants of regionalization were a key part
of his strategy. The 1972 Addis Ababa peace deal was one of the most
successful, winning him a huge, if short-lived, southern constituency. In
1981, as economic pressure on his regime mounted, he sought new allies.
The 1981 Regional Government Act, which almost brought about the
return of the Kafia Kingi enclave to Bahr al-Ghazal (see Chapter 6), was
one of Nimeiri's attempts to reshuffle power structures in the hinterland
in order to manage crises at the centre of the state. The Act was partly
intended to enable Nimeiri to deal with any change in southern loyalties
by creating five large political units in the north that could counterbalance the unified southern regional government, which was itself soon
to be divided up.

Al-Tom al-Nur, the Fertit leader who went on to lead a Khartoum-
sponsored militia in the second civil war in the south, was an SSU official
in Wau in the early 1980s. Many leaders in Raga at the time supported the
idea of dividing up Southern Sudan. Al-Tom al-Nur was one:

> [After the 1972 Addis Ababa peace deal, in Nimeiri's time]
> I was deputy secretary of the Sudan Socialist Union in Wau.
> Bahr al-Ghazal was one region [with a Dinka majority]. We
> suffered a lot from Dinka imperialism, and we asked Nimeiri

to give us our own province. They gave us a province in Wau
and Raga in 1984 [in fact in 1983], with Ali Tamim Fartak as
the first governor. We could do political work in Raga, far
from the SPLM, to remove Abel Alier [then president of the
HEC, of Dinka origin]. Abel Alier's idea was to take Raga and
make it part of Aweil, put Tonj with Wau. After 50 years Fertit
would be no more. They would all marry Dinkas. We studied
this whole issue. We worked with contacts in Equatoria to
divide up the HEC.[97]

At the time, the state promoted the development of ethnic consciousness in Southern Sudan by shifting borders. In 1983, Nimeiri moved to
replace the HEC with three southern provinces, abrogating the Addis
Ababa agreement and its federal arrangements. Southern dissatisfac-
tions and disorder immediately turned into armed rebellion. This was
the start of the second civil war, which is described in more detail in the
next chapter.

Many people of Raga county supported redivision (a policy associated
with Equatorian politicians), motivated by a fear of engulfment by Dinka
and Nuer groups, and a sense that some Dinka politicians had misused
the opportunities of peace. Smaller groups were set to benefit from the
proliferation of local posts that redivision implied. The 1983 redivision
was unlike the Southern Policy of 1930 because it aimed at creating differences and weakness within an emerging southern political community,
rather than separating Southerners from northerners, or 'Arabs' from
'Africans'. But there were also important similarities with the 1930 policy.
At a time of economic crisis, the state was using differences between
people in order to control the periphery and extract its wealth with very
little investment. Changing administrative boundaries was a low-cost
way for the state to create small rewards for local constituencies, and to
play one constituency off against another.

....

[97] Interview with al-Tom al-Nur, SAF major general and leader of the Peace Forces
militia, 1984–2006, May 2010.

In Darfur, by contrast, the government had been pursuing an unsuccessful policy of aggregation rather than fragmentation: a bigger Darfur to counterbalance the south. Changes to regional boundaries coincided with changing policies on tribal authority, or Native Administration—the colonial- and Mahdist-era tribal leaders who were reconstituted as tax-collectors and low-cost administrators with judicial and executive powers. Parliamentary regimes began scrutinizing their powers in the 1960s, and Nimeiri replaced them with local party structures in the early 1970s, at the height of modernizing optimism. This happened at a time of enormous social upheaval. The droughts of the 1970s contributed to huge southward migrations of northern groups who were giving up a historical association with camel-keeping and seeking urban or agrarian livelihoods—many of these migrants came to the goz lands just north of Radom. Sudan's economic crash came a few years later: in Darfur, this combined with new droughts to create widespread famine (de Waal, 1989, pp. 70–71). Incidences of armed robbery spread in the province, and many people believed that the replacement of tribal leaders by officials of Nimeiri's SSU had limited the authorities' ability to deal with such breakdowns of social discipline (Ibrahim, 2008, pp. 153–73). But droughts, migration and the strangulation of economic alternatives, such as the WSP, also played a role, and as pressure on livelihoods increased, suspicion and enmity between ethnic groups grew. Habbaniya people in South Darfur, for example, respected the adaptability of Zaghawa groups, who had switched from pastoralism to peripheral agriculture and were finding their way into urban markets. But they also associated them with armed robbery:

> Zaghawa made a transition, compelled by drought. They
> had two choices, urban migration or robbery. They went to
> Nyala and Suq Libya and were successful. The robbery system
> contributed to [Darfur's 2003] civil war.[98]

....

[98] Interview with Habbaniya person, name and place withheld, May 2010.

Islamization and a divided periphery

In 1983, a few months after Nimeiri divided up the south, he introduced Islamic law in northern Sudan. With this move he trumped his Islamist allies and competitors and garnered support from the established populations of northern cities, which were becoming inundated with migrants escaping the economic crisis in rural Sudan. In Darfur, drought and the movement of drought-impoverished people had led to outbreaks of armed robbery: attacks on rural markets and lorries were cast in Islamic terms as the crime of *hiraba*, or waging war against God and his prophet and spreading corruption and violence. For such crimes the Quran mandates punishment by death, crucifixion or cross-amputation of foot and hand—punishments that were included in a theatrical new penal code (*Quran*, 5: 33).

The emergence of Islamism at the centre of Sudan coincided with a re-concentration of power in Khartoum. The regime increasingly managed regions in the periphery by shuffling ethnic alliances and using changes to administrative boundaries as an alternative to the investment of real resources. Peripheral peoples seeking to benefit from the state's resources would increasingly have to identify with the state's Islamist ideology—many Zaghawa people, for example, became involved in Islamist commercial and political networks in the national capital.

In Fertit-land, one of the most Islamized areas of Southern Sudan, the Islamization of the centre was tied into the ethnicization of the periphery. Nimeiri needed to divide the south in order to deal with dramatic changes at the centre of his regime, and Fertit people's differences were useful for him. Some felt antagonized by what they perceived as domination of political and military posts by Nilotic groups, particularly neighbouring Dinka people. They called for changes to administrative boundaries and supported the redivision of the south as a means to gain government posts. The Muslim beliefs and culture of some Fertit groups probably helped them gain concessions.

Some Muslim Fertit leaders of the period reportedly proposed to Nimeiri that Fertit-land become part of Darfur. Islamist politicians amongst the Fertit went on to claim that Raga county would be the route through which Islam would come to Southern Sudan.[99] This was to become a key cause of the civil war that was set off by the redivision of Southern Sudan, and is the subject of the following chapter.

[99] Interviews with Raga people, names withheld, March and April 2010.

9.   Civil war in Southern Sudan, 1983–2005

In the 1960s, Fertit people in Raga county joined the first rebellion in post-independence Southern Sudan, but when the second rebellion began, many Fertit enlisted in a pro-Khartoum militia. This chapter examines why this militia was popular, and why the SPLA failed to mobilize the area for the first 18 years of the war. The reason lies largely in the relationship between government and SPLM constituencies in Fertit-land and in Darfur: the government's logistical capabilities, and its promotion of localism and Islamism, proved a more successful mix than the SPLA's shaky supply lines and appeals to inclusion. But in 2001, the SPLA was able to take over Raga briefly and polarize the population of the county, setting in motion a round of displacements on a scale not previously seen in the war.

The start of the war and the Fertit response

In 1983, the Khartoum government's moves towards the dissolution of the Regional Government in Juba signalled the start of a new civil war and the formation of the SPLA. Its leaders sought to establish a credible and unitary military force early, in order to avoid the political divisions of the previous civil war. But it faced the same problem as Anyanya in terms of local mobilization: people were organized around tribe and language groups, and tribal identification appeared to have deepened during the Addis Ababa peace period. Al-Tom al-Nur, who set up a Fertit-based militia that would become one the SPLA's main enemies in Bahr al-Ghazal, refused what he felt was a threatening invitation:

In 1983 when the SPLM started the war, the Dinka tribes
asked the Fertit in Western Bahr al-Ghazal to join them in the
rebellion. Retired Major Nyoung Diu was in the SSU, he said,
if you don't join us in the movement we will send you [back]
to Central Africa. I thought, we will make militias [to oppose
them]. In August 1984 I set them up to defend citizens. I
became commander of the Peace Forces.[100]

The Peace Forces were one of the first militias of the war. In the SPLA's
view, they were key strategic forces for three reasons:

- they controlled the supply line from the north to a major garrison
  in Wau;

- they promoted localist and tribalist views of Southern Sudan
  which, in the SPLA's view, stood in the way of their challenge to
  the centralising power of Khartoum;

- their base lay in partially Islamized tribes, who were seen by
  the Khartoum government as a means to spread their religious
  ideology in the south.[101]

The SPLA opened the war in Western Bahr al-Ghazal with attacks on
perceived allies of the northern government within the south. Between
1985 and 1987, the rebels came down the road from Aweil, in the flood
plain, to attack the most Islamized groups in Fertit-land, the Njagulgule
and Feroghe tribes. During the first civil war, Njagulgule and Feroghe
people had not been forcibly moved from their homes.[102] But today,
twenty-five years after the attacks that started the second civil war, many
of them are still displaced in Raga.[103] SPLA attacks on Fertit areas were

....

[100] Interview with al-Tom al-Nur, SAF major general and leader of the Peace Forces
militia, 1984–2006, May 2010.
[101] Interview with senior SPLA officers, names and place withheld, June 2010.
[102] Interviews with Raga people, names withheld, March 2010.
[103] Interviews with members of tribes in Raga, March 2010; interview with al-Tom al-Nur,
SAF major general and leader of the Peace Forces militia, 1984–2006, May 2010.

part of a strategy in the mid-1980s to attack civilian populations seen as hostile, which was partially due to the inability of the guerrillas to hold territory (Johnson, 2007, p. 83). Attacks on Raga at Christmastime in 1987 and on villages on the road from Wau to Deim Zubeir, caused widespread displacement (Sudan Transition and Recovery Database, 2003). But on the whole, SPLA commanders were not able to mount operations along the highly strategic supply line for Wau, which ran through Raga. Even their reconnaissance parties fell foul of the Peace Forces.[104]

Government forces controlled the road from Raga to Wau. SPLA attacks against civilians helped the government co-opt the area's population, most of whom joined the Peace Forces. In Wau, the ethnic politics of the 1980s had divided the city between Fertit people and Dinka and Jur-Luo people. Each had their own side of town and their own markets. They even had their own security forces: Al-Tom al-Nur's forces were overwhelmingly Fertit, and the government police were largely Dinka. In 1987, these polarizations led to massacres on the streets. When the Wau army garrison was under the command of Major General Abu Gurun tensions between Fertit and Dinka people reached what many interviewees reported was their worst point.

> Dinkas and Fertit fighting was caused by Abu Gurun. It was
> three days war, among Dinka and non-Dinka. Fertit were
> in the Peace Forces and Dinka were people of SPLA. Abu
> Gurun supplied Fertit with ammunition and guns and also
> supplied Dinka with ammunition and guns. To see who is the
> strongest. Wau was divided into two. East part was Dinka and
> Jur [Jur-Luo]. West part was Fertit.[105]

Peace came only after Abu Gurun was removed. A Dinka governor, George Kongor Arop, organized reconciliation meetings in Wau. Ten years later in 1998, an SPLA attack on the town led the government to

....

[104] Interview with senior SPLA officers, Juba, June 2010.
[105] Interview with Wau resident, name withheld, February 2010.

deploy the Peace Forces once again to attack unarmed people, identified as rebels because of their ethnicity, resulting in massacres and lynchings (Human Rights Watch, 1999).

The Peace Forces recruitment in the 1980s

In Raga county, people from all the different Fertit groups joined the Peace Forces as volunteers in the second civil war. But support for these forces was not universal: one Peace Forces officer stated that the militia was involved in killings of suspected SPLA supporters. Some Dinka people, seen as ethnic allies of the SPLA, were also killed by the Peace Forces.[106] In Raga county the Peace Forces were local intermediaries of the government army, protecting Fertit people from the kind of all-out war occurring in the flood plains of Bahr al-Ghazal. There, the government had recruited militias from Kordofanian and Darfurian Baggara elements to secure its lines of communications through a scorched-earth policy that caused widespread devastation. In keeping the SPLA at bay in Raga county, the militia prevented a repeat of the enormous displacements of the first civil war.

The existence of the Peace Forces, as a government militia with wide local participation, ensured that, in Raga, militarized Baggara elements did not engage in the kind of violence witnessed in the flood plain to the east. Their commander, al-Tom al-Nur, intended the Forces to act as vectors of Arab and Muslim influence in the south. Al-Nur recruited Fellata, Habbaniya and Rizeigat fighters early on, believing that support from more Arabized or Islamized groups would strengthen his position. Some recruits were northerners living in Western Bahr al-Ghazal, but al-Nur also took his recruitment campaign north:

> In 1984... I became the commander of the National Sudanese
> Peace Forces. Because we in the Fertit are small, I thought
> we should get some of the Arab nationalities, Rizeigat and

....

[106] Interview with former Peace Forces officer, name and place withheld, March 2010.

Habbaniya, so we could be strong. I went from Wau to El
Daein [in South Darfur] and Muglad [his mother's home
in Kordofan], I said you're my mother's family, help me.
Throughout the war the SPLM could not enter the area. We
had 66 camps, six brigades... I was commander, elected in a
two-way election. I won because people saw that I have Arab
elements and southern roots. I knew Omar al-Bashir when
he was a colonel. I'm Muslim, I can get the north involved. In
1984 the Arabs joined the Peace Forces. Taysha and Rizeigat
were with us, but we had only two Habbaniya. There were
a lot of Fallata. I got a lot of information from them. I gave
them a lot of arms.[107]

Military recruits in the economically stressed Baggara lands, especially
those for unpaid tribal militias, often came from poor, settled families,
with mothers or grandparents who had origins in Bahr al-Ghazal. The
incorporation of these soldiers into a Fertit-led force recalled the cross-
border military alliances of the slave trade and the Mahdiya. But the idea
of Darfur people of southern lineage returning to the south to fight for
the Khartoum government was one that caused the SPLA a great deal of
unease. One senior SPLA officer commented:

Most informers and most people who have no mercy in the
Popular Defence Forces (PDF, a militia formation) were the
Southern Sudanese, who went and migrated to northern
Sudan and settled in Fallata and Habbaniya areas. Some of
them are even known from their clans in Aweil. They could
not catch up—go to school—they went to Quranic schools.
They were used to command PDF operations in the south.[108]

....

[107] Interview with al-Tom al-Nur, Khartoum, May 2010.
[108] Interview with senior SPLA officer, name and location withheld, June 2010.

The Ingaz regime: militias and ethnicity in Darfur and Bahr al-Ghazal in 1989

The military dictatorship of Gaafar Nimeiri fell in 1985. In 1986 a parliamentary regime was established after general elections in which the National Islamic Front, the main Islamist party, won about one sixth of the vote. It gained only two southern seats: one was in Bahr al-Ghazal, won by Ali Tamim Fartak, a member of the leading Feroghe family who was the governor of the Western Bahr al-Ghazal *mudiriya* (province, equivalent of a British district or state of today) that had been established in 1983 (Chinyankandath, 1991, p. 86). When the Ingaz regime came to power in a coup in 1989, Fartak played a leading role.

The Ingaz used Islamist language to promote the intensification of the war in the south: some regime elements declared the war to be a jihad or struggle for the faith (de Waal and Abdel Salam, 2004, p. 72). The government's Islamist orientation influenced military mobilization: the parliamentary regime in Khartoum had begun to mobilize tribal militias in northern Sudan in the mid-1980s, using religious appeals to recruit forces. In 1989, one of the first legislative acts of the Ingaz was to recognize the Popular Defence Forces (PDF) as an umbrella body for northern tribal militias. The PDF was extended to create an urban militia, as well as recruiting in rural northern Sudan. Some of al-Tom al-Nur's officers went to Darfur to set up the PDF there, but the Peace Forces, as a southern militia, were never part of the PDF:

> When I came to Omar al-Bashir in August 1989 he said we
> should join the PDF, I said, we have lots of Christians, PDF is
> for Muslims. I won't go in with them, but we can cooperate
> on operations. They took Misseriya and Rizeigat officers from
> Peace Forces to make the PDF in Muglad and El Daein. The
> government treated PDF better than Peace Forces, the PDF
> were like the children of their own wombs, they had heavy
> weapons. Peace Forces got no salary, they worked for free...
> they were making money from the convoys. They took my

> Rizeigat and Misseriya soldiers and said, 'You're Arabs and
> you work with Fertit?'

Tribal and religious affiliations were becoming central to the militarized politics of the periphery.

The SPLM's alternative vision, and its 1991 split

The SPLM offered an alternative ideology to the fragmentation and subordination of the periphery implied by the tribal militia policy: a New Sudan that included the peoples of Sudan's vast, diverse and impoverished margins, replacing the political, economic and cultural dominance of the elites and their constituencies in the northern Nile valley. For a mix of pragmatic and ideological reasons, the SPLM wanted a united and transformed Sudan, and sought to mobilize people in Darfur and other parts of northern Sudan. But in some respects it was wrong-footed by the Ingaz regime's appeals to tribalism and Islam, which may have been more comprehensible to the people of the area than a SPLM's vision of the New Sudan, explained in the 1980s through a lumbering version of the Ethiopian Marxist curriculum. 'Teaching Marxist philosophy and hard dialectics to peasants and secondary school drop-outs was the surest way of creating counter-revolutionaries,' comments the SPLM's most supple Marxist thinker (Nyaba, 2000, p. 54).

An example of the inapplicability of the New Sudan vision to everyday realities became all too clear in an incident in the Kara settlement of Minamba. In 1991, Daud Bolad, an erstwhile Darfurian Islamist who had defected to the SPLA, fought his way up the road to Kafia Kingi to take the armed struggle to Darfur. It was the SPLA's most convincing attempt to bring Darfur into its war against Khartoum, a development that would have pressured the centre by linking the struggles and disaffections of two peripheries. At Minamba, he encountered the Kara chief Abu Ras Qurawa, who was carrying an obsolete rifle.

> Chief Abu Ras was hit during the movement of Daud Bolad.
> Bolad killed him because he was carrying a weapon; he was

carrying a Lee-Enfield rifle. All chiefs in the south got one for protection.[109]

The killing may have been a misunderstanding, but it alienated the Kara from the SPLM. Bolad continued up the road to Darfur but the SPLA did not have the supply lines to support his campaign.[110] The government mobilized Baggara groups to capture him, including a militia from the Beni Halba group, who were based around a town called Id al-Ghanam (meaning 'watering-place of the goats' in Arabic). As a reward for the group's support, the government renamed the town Id al-Fursan (meaning 'watering-place of the knights'). The incident was a striking example of the drift towards ethnic conflict in Darfur and also of the financial straits of the government, reduced to rewarding its supporters with rhetorical decorations for fighting their neighbours.[111]

Chief Abu Ras's killing may have been an accident of war, but in the long view it was a critical error of the SPLM not to be able to mobilize ethnic groups like the Kara, which were spread out across Sudan. It was also a critical error to fail in Darfur. It is noteworthy that the only historical example of a successful military strategy to reshape Sudan's centre from its periphery was the Mahdist revolution—which fought its way to Khartoum from the west with armies from South Darfur and Bahr al-Ghazal (including a large Kara army).

After 1991, divisions within the SPLM made military enterprises of Bolad's kind impossible. Several SPLM leaders who wanted the movement to fight for southern independence, rather than for the New Sudan that Bolad had failed to achieve, set up their own armed factions. These factions were configured around ethnicity: most but not all SPLM dissident leaders were Nuer, and, with some important exceptions, they recruited Nuer militias.

The SPLM ceded the area west of Wau to the Khartoum government.

....

[109] Interview with Kara people, Minamba, March 2010.
[110] Interview with senior SPLA officers, names and location withheld, June 2010.
[111] Interview with Ahmed Diraige, governor of Darfur 1980–83, October 2009.

The intensification of ethnic politics in the south sometimes benefited the political leaders of smaller groups such as Fertit ones. But Fertit leaders could lose out when ethnic alliances shifted. In 1997, six different southern parties and factions that had split from the SPLM signed an agreement with the government which became known as the Khartoum Peace Agreement (KPA). Most of these parties and factions were linked to militias drawn from Nuer and Dinka groups—no Fertit took part. The KPA involved the reappointment of governors in southern states. Thus Ali Tamim Fartak, from the Feroghe leading family, was replaced as governor by Charles Julu, a politician from a Nilotic group (Human Rights Watch, 1999). The Council of the South, the southern government set up by the KPA, had only one Fertit member.[112]

The Khartoum government developed a peace strategy called 'Peace From Within', intended as a set of local agreements across the south. These aimed to put down the many local rebellions generated by the regime's long policy of fostering ethnic division. In Raga county, some Fertit chiefs were taken to Khartoum and encouraged to develop local peace talks. According to several of these chiefs, they then approached the SPLA in Northern Bahr al-Ghazal and were invited to a peace conference. Many Fertit chiefs were arrested, however, and taken to SPLA areas in Western Equatoria. Binga chief Abd al-Rahman Dahia from Minamba joined the talks, and was imprisoned in Maridi in Western Equatoria, where, it is said, he died from stress and hunger.[113]

The SPLA attack on Raga in 2001, and widespread displacement

The SPLA mounted another assault on Raga town in 2001. The attack was aimed both at controlling Raga county, which would allow the

....

[112] Interview with Arkangelo Musa Albino, NCP president and former commissioner of Raga county 2000–05, Raga, March 2010.

[113] Interviews with chiefs involved in the Peace From Within meetings, names and places withheld, March 2010.

SPLA to threaten Darfur, and at polarizing Fertit society. Most Fertit groups participated in the Peace Forces, and the SPLA intended to force people to choose sides, helping the SPLM to identify a Fertit constituency of support. Under the command of Rizig Zakaria (a member of the Ngbongbo or Kresh Hofra group who was later commissioner of Raga and is now governor of Western Bahr al-Ghazal) the SPLA captured and held Raga and the roads to Timsah and Boro Medina for the whole of the 2001 rainy season.

Nearly the entire population of the county was displaced in the events that followed. When the SPLA arrived, 18,500 people fled to Radom and towns in South Darfur (Sudan Transition and Recovery Database, 2003). The government responded ferociously, deploying PDF militias drawn from Baggara tribes in South Darfur who were part of a predatory war economy that targeted the Dinka and Nuer borderlands in Bahr al-Ghazal and Upper Nile. This brought the burning and looting warfare that had come to characterize those Dinka and Nuer areas to Raga county. The retreating SPLA warned the population of this, and when they retreated, people who had not gone to Darfur fled to the forests, to SPLA areas of Equatoria and to CAR.

When those who had gone to Darfur returned in 2002 the area had been successfully polarized. The 2001 attack meant that just about every

FIGURE 6.
WEALTH GROUPS IN RAGA BEFORE 2001

Wealth Group	Estimated proportion of population (%)	Estimated annual food income before 2001	Estimated annual cash income before 2001	
Better	15	Produce 30–45 bags of cereals, own 20–30 goats and 5-6 cows	SDD 70,000	USD 273
Middle	30	Produce 20–25 bags of cereals, own 10–15 goats	SDD 17,500	USD 68
Poor	55	Produce 12–15 bags of cereals, own 5–10 goats	SDD 13,200	USD 51

Source: Sudan Transition and Recovery Database (2003).

person in Raga had a personal experience of displacement. Peace Forces soldiers who had stayed in Raga changed sides and joined the SPLA and went to fight in other fronts across Southern Sudan. Some people had to run from both armies: the population of the Kara village of Minamba, for example, fled both the SPLA and the PDF counter-attack.[114]

Prior to 2001 Raga county people had been displaced by SPLA attacks on the Feroghe and Njagulgule areas in the 1980s. Since those attacks had ended, population movement had been motivated by the economic stress and inequality of a war economy based on levies on convoys, which went to Peace Forces commanders. The many armies of the area made demands on the local population for food.[115] Women and girls living in Raga were drawn into prostitution or extra-marital relationships around the barracks, an indication of family separations and social breakdown: a UN study estimated that in 2003, 15–20 per cent of the households were headed by women, most of them in the poorest groups.[116] Other UN studies looking at the period before the 2001 displacements found stark disparities in wealth between poorer and richer groups, and an increase in dependence on wild foods, a sign that farming was not able to meet household needs (Sudan Transition and Recovery Database, 2003). All groups were deeply impoverished by displacement.

The Fertit experience of displacement after 2001 was, in some respects, shorter lived than that of people who came from the scorched earth zones of the Nilotic flood plain. In other respects, the Fertit experience was further reaching. Most of the population, which had lived through two centuries of almost constant harassment and displacement, was moved once more. This move was different to previous ones because so many Fertit people now had urban connections in the north and south. It was the beginning of an oil boom in Khartoum, and Fertit people who moved there may decide to stay. Fertit associations that include established

....

[114] Interviews with people in Raga and Minamba, March 2010.

[115] Interview with chief, name and place withheld, March 2010.

[116] Interviews with Raga people, names withheld, March 2010; Sudan Transition and Recovery Database, 2003.

Fertit residents and new arrivals have been established to provide financial support and a calendar of celebrations. Many of the new arrivals take
advantage of the opportunities, as one long-standing Kresh resident of
Khartoum explains:

> Academically those who came from the south have achieved
> much more. You can acquire skills, you will not get the
> opportunity again. People who live here are mostly labourers,
> blacksmiths. People from south are very interested in
> education.[117]

Most people who fled to SPLA areas did not return to Raga until 2006,
a year after the CPA was signed. As noted in Chapter 7, the SPLA
commander in Western Equatoria improved the road from Tembura to
Deim Zubeir, in order to prevent Raga people returning through Bahr
al-Ghazal's capital Wau and settling there. It may have been an indication of the SPLM's sense that it needed to muster a constituency in
Raga, whose people, in 2005, were all former internally displaced persons
(IDPs) from Darfur. But it was also an indication that Fertit leaders saw
urbanization as an unstoppable trend in Fertit society, once associated
with mobile forest livelihoods.

The ceasefire in Bahr al-Ghazal

The CPA brought a ceasefire between the SPLA and the government
army in 2005. For the first two years of the peace agreement, security
in the area was managed by the Joint Integrated Units (JIU), a military
structure established by the CPA which brought together personnel from
both armies under a unified command. In other border areas, the JIUs
were sometimes implicated in ceasefire breaches, but in Raga county, no
breaches occurred—the JIUs were dominated by Peace Forces personnel,
and their local character may have improved security. The SPLA did

---

[117] Interview with Lutfi Muhammad Wadatalla, intellectual from a Hofrat al-Nahas
family, Khartoum, April 2010.

not deploy in Raga county until two years later as it was too much of a logistical challenge to do so more quickly. People called them 'SPLA proper' when they arrived, to distinguish them from the small SPLA contingents in the JIUs. The SPLA's takeover from the JIUs was a smooth one, although there appears to have been no joint planning between the two armies. But the arrival of the SPLA marked a shift from a security regime based on a local militia, to a multi-ethnic army with a national agenda.

A second ceasefire agreement, which has in retrospect proved more inviolable (the CPA has survived four serious breaches), came with the Juba Declaration of January 2006—an agreement that incorporated into the SPLA most of the ethnic militias that were formerly aligned with Khartoum. Al-Tom al-Nur refused incorporation, but 5,000 of his troops accepted it, along with 2,025 Rizeigat and other Baggara troops from the Peace Forces. The Juba Declaration is evidence of a change in SPLM thinking. Former adversaries now serve in mixed SPLA units, and militias are deployed outside their home areas (SPLA brigades in Raga include many Nuer troops). The costs of the Declaration have been huge—about half the GoSS budget goes on security, possibly more—but it may offer Southern Sudan a route to national unity in the way that the Peace Forces provided some unity to the people of Raga county. A senior SPLA officer noted in an interview:

> [The SPLA is] an example that can bring the people of South
> Sudan together—we have all representation within the SPLA
> together. And we've opened up. Whatever damage you have
> done to SPLA you are forgivable. When you come you are
> transformed.[118]

The Peace Forces may have helped reshape Fertit identities, and now some in the SPLA believe that the army can generate a multi-ethnic southern identity. Using military structures to perform political and

....

[118] Interview with senior SPLA officers, names and location withheld, June 2010.

cultural tasks has many risks. These risks were acknowledged by senior SPLA officers in interviews, even though they recognize that this kind of militarization is inevitable.

> If lead sector is military, it has a lot of implications for society. We're aware of that. We are forced by the north to do that. North has decided to form militias. They are depleting our resources through those militias, whether fighting them or integrating them.[119]

[119] Interview with senior SPLA officers, names and location withheld, June 2010.

10. Civil war in Darfur's southern borderlands

In 1930, the people of Kafia Kingi were moved or escaped to the banks of the Umbelacha, the southern edge of Goz Dango, as the British established a cultural barrier along the Bahr al-Arab/Kiir River, which aimed to isolate the south from northern and Muslim influence. Forty years later, in the 1970s, drought migrants from North Darfur began arriving in Goz Dango, just when the agricultural potential of its sandy soils had been transformed by borehole technology. But within a decade, a clutch of inter-related crises in Darfur's ecology, agricultural production and the international economy fragmented the region's political order, leading to two decades of instability, and eventually to a war which broke out in 2003. This chapter looks at how the war in South Darfur set the different groups of Goz Dango against each other in violence that sent refugees fleeing from Darfur into Bahr al-Ghazal.

Peace along the Umbelacha River in the 1970s and 1980s

Kara and Binga people were caught up in the ethnic politics of Bahr al-Ghazal in the 1990s, when the chiefs of both groups died at the hands of the SPLA, although one of these deaths may well have been an accident of war. A hundred years earlier, both these groups had taken part in the Mahdiya; both have links with Jebel Marra in Darfur and with Ouanda Jallé in what is now CAR; and both originally came to the Kafia Kingi area around the end of the Darfur sultanate, in 1913. In 1930, the British decided to move them to Minamba, on the road from Boro Medina to Raga, as part of their Southern Policy. But many of them fled across the Umbelacha River, into Darfur, where they lived in river-bank villages perched on the end of Goz Dango, the westernmost goz of Darfur.

Until the 1970s, Goz Dango was an empty place. Borehole technology in the 1960s greatly improved the agricultural potential of the easily-worked soil of the areas. And the droughts of the 1970s and 1980s brought people from North Darfur and the borders with Chad to work the lands there. Many of these migrants were from pastoralist groups like the Zaghawa, adapting to new livelihoods in response to what appeared to be long-term climate change. And there was the promise of agricultural investment in the area: the Zaghawa move had been facilitated by the government, and international donors were studying the goz as a place to develop smallholder rainfed agriculture 'in the interests of equity' (NA/OD/20/524). Relations between the Zaghawa incomers, older inhabitants from the Kafia Kingi enclave, and the traditional custodians of the land, the Habbaniya traditional authorities, all appeared to be very good. But three decades later, in 2003, a civil war began in Darfur and in 2006, it pitted Zaghawa people against Habbaniya, and Kara people against Binga, in some of the most terrifying acts of violence witnessed in the Darfur conflict.

The roots of Darfur's fragmentation, 1981–2003

Differences between Darfurian people emerged over time. In 1981, Nimeiri's government combined the provinces of North and South Darfur into a single region. This seems to have been an attempt to create a regional counterweight to the autonomous south, a prelude to the division of the south in 1983, which precipitated the second civil war. The majority of the population in the new single region of Darfur were Fur people, who made up a minority in each of the two provinces. Darfurians identifying as Arabs began to resist perceived domination by Fur groups.

Drought, widespread migration and a Libyan war in Chad that polarized Arab and non-Arab identities and sent millions of refugees into Darfur all increased the salience of ethnicity in the region's politics. In the 1980s these factors contributed to the outbreak of fighting between Fur and Arab groups—the backdrop for the defection of Daud Bolad (a Fur) to the SPLA. They also contributed to a catastrophic famine in the 1980s, which was compounded by wider economic pressure on Sudan (de Waal, 1989). Nimeiri's government abolished traditional authorities such as the Habbaniya nazirate in the 1970s, a policy partly aimed at promoting the development of supra-tribal identities, but in practice often complicating relationships between different groups, especially in stressed areas where robbery, rather than agriculture, was the chosen adaptation strategy for migrants (Ibrahim, 2008, pp. 163ff). When Nimeiri's government fell, the brief parliamentary regime that succeeded his introduced new powers for chiefs in 'backward' or border areas—solidifying the distinctions between urban and rural Sudan (Ibrahim, 2008, pp. 239ff).

The current Ingaz government in Sudan, which overthrew the parliamentary regime, went further. After coming to power in 1989 it largely cut off investment to Darfur and other peripheral areas, as part of a stabilization programme aimed at servicing international debt and curbing inflation, which was over 100 per cent a year in the early 1990s.[120] It broke Darfur up into three states in 1994, and gave relatively powerless state governments responsibility for service delivery. The regime was creating a dominant, commercial centre that was responsive to international financial systems, overseas markets for Sudanese labour and the global trade economy. At the same time, it was cutting administrative costs in the periphery and to do so, it needed to dismantle larger political communities that might have provided an alternative. States replaced regions, political parties and religious sects were abolished or divided, and tribal structures were reinvented. Militias revolutionized the tribes internally, empowering violent, entrepreneurial young men against their elders, and tensions between tribes were aggravated by aligning existing administrative boundaries with tribal territories. The resulting proliferation of tribally defined administrative units created a crisis, according to a local government expert from Buram:

....

[120] Figures for investment in the periphery in the 1970s in El Shibly (1990, p. 58); figures for 1990s in African Development Bank (1998, p. 25); World Bank (2003, pp. 46, 52).

The dynamics of tribalism created by the above-mentioned administrative divisions will help explain the devastating conflicts amongst all tribes in South Darfur over the boundaries of these new [administrative] units... not a single tribe in South Darfur is not engaged with its neighbors in the boundary issue (Takana, 2008, p. 10).

In 2005–06, the government in Nyala produced a list of tribal reconciliation conferences it had sponsored. It was a time of war, and these conferences were only organized for groups linked to the government's allies—the conferences obviously did not deal with rebel divisions. In Buram locality, the list shows how chaotic relations were between government allies (see Figure 7). These conflicts were not being organized by the government: instead, Buram locality was living through all the contradictions of a neglected periphery, where ethnicity was sometimes manipulated to establish government control.

FIGURE 7.
GOVERNMENT-SPONSORED RECONCILIATION CONFERENCES
IN BURAM LOCALITY IN 2005–06

Date	Conflicting groups
Mar '05	Habbaniya and Rizeigat
May '05	Habbaniya and Masalat
Jan '06	Fellata, Habbaniya, Masalat, Mahadi, Rizeigat
Apr '06	Habbaniya, Fellata
Jun '06	Habbaniya, Fellata
Aug '06	Habbaniya, Rizeigat
Dec '06	Binga, Kara

Notes: Until 2009, Kafia Kingi was part of Buram locality.
Source: Takana (2008, p. 3).

The outbreak of war in Darfur, from 2003

The NCP's management of the peripheral areas of the country also involved systems of patronage at the level of education and state employment Political support was often a condition of university entrance or credit. But a split in the Islamist movement in the late 1990s undermined the NCP system—and many of the Darfurians who had joined the state apparatus were associated with the losing side of the split. Islamism lost the political initiative in Darfur, but the main alternative—an alliance between Darfur and the south—did not emerge. One reason was that by 2002 the SPLM had begun serious peace talks with the government: Darfur was excluded from the agenda. Oil exports from southern fields were beginning. Darfur's exclusion from these developments was a major factor that pushed two decades of instability there into open insurgency.

The rebel groups in Darfur were drawn largely from Fur, Masalit and Zaghawa groups, who spoke Nilo-Saharan languages as well as Arabic. In response, the government mobilized militias from the most ecologically beleaguered Arabic-speaking groups to carry out a scorched-earth policy against the ethnic constituencies of the rebels. These included landless camel-herders of the far north, sometimes collectively called Rizeigat because they shared some section names with the cattle-herding Rizeigat of the south. Government-controlled militias from these groups helped to force millions of Darfurians into displaced camps

Both government and rebels in Darfur presented the war in the language of ethnicity. They were assisted by outside observers and advocates, many of whom had become accustomed to looking for ethnic victims and perpetrators as a means to simplify and explain the deepening insecurity of the global periphery. And all three groups transposed onto Darfur the ethnic divisions of the civil war between the south and the centre, presenting Darfur as a conflict between Arabs and Africans.

In South Darfur, the region's most populous state, the reality was different. Up to 2003, elements from the large Baggara population, particularly Rizeigat Baggara, had been fighting in government PDF militias, attacking communities in SPLM-controlled areas of the south. But they were able to resist government pressure to get involved in the war in Darfur. Indeed, when the civil war ended with the CPA's 2005 ceasefire, some militarized Baggara elements joined the SPLA.

This did not mean, however, that South Darfur was a peaceful place, or that it avoided the drift towards racial and tribal forms of identification in the rest of the region. Goz Dango, for example, saw fighting over land throughout the 1990s. This was linked to policies that promoted groups identifying as Arab (principally the Habbaniya group) over other, smaller groups. This affected everyday relationships in Habbaniya areas, including Buram locality and the Kafia Kingi enclave in the south-western corner of South Darfur. A leader from one small tribe in Buram locality area described the tone of mocking submission he adopted when talking to members of Arab tribes: 'We call them *dawal istikbar* [imperialist states], and they get happy when we say that. Sometimes they say "you haven't given me my full title" if you forget.'[121]

In Radom, the administrative centre adjacent to the Kafia Kingi enclave, tensions emerged between the Awlad Arab groups whom the British had identified as northerners, and the Kara, Binga and Dongo groups, who were sometimes identified with the south.

> Until the 1970s and 1980s people were living in peace and nobody asked about your tribe. My father's best friends were from the south and they were like brothers... Then there were problems. It was not something you could see—people from the southern tribes wanted their own umda, Dongo, Kara, Binga—they felt some provocation from Awlad Arab, lack of recognition of others. They were not Muslims. They had *kujur* [traditional African beliefs]. People started to say things like *abid* [slave].[122]

....

[121] Interview with tribal leader, name and place withheld, April 2010.
[122] Interview with Radom citizen, name and place withheld, May 2010.

In 2003, increased ethnic tensions pushed Buram locality into conflict. The drought migrants who came to south-west Darfur in the 1970s included many Zaghawa people, one of the largest non-Arab groups in Darfur. Initially, Habbaniya authorities had welcomed them to Buram's remote Goz Dango, which came under their control. In the 1980s, more migrants came to work as labourers on the successful farms that the 1970s migrants had established: Masalit, Tama, Erenga, Gimir, Masalati, Misseriya Jebel—all fitting into the 'African' side of Darfur's popular new racial schema.

After the 2003 mutiny, rebel groups such as the Justice and Equality Movement (JEM) tried to raise support, especially funds, from these relatively well-off farmers.

> JEM established an office in Gereida and began to recruit Tama and Erenga and other groups in the Goz Dango; Minni Minawi [then a leader of the SLA] was in far north but started mobilizing in the area. They had money—in the north, a family could not pay half a million [Sudanese pounds, about USD 200], but in the south a small guy could pay that. The idea was to use tribal structures for fundraising.[123]

Gereida, a town to the east of Buram locality with many drought migrants, became the focus of a contest between rebel groups divided by ethnicity. Zaghawa groups fought Masalit groups for control of the town, alerting the Habbaniya leaders to the troubles in their area. They began mobilizing their own private armies—these were not government-controlled, although the government sometimes supplied them with arms. Militias associated with Zaghawa groups killed the brother of the Habbaniya nazir in an ambush.

The crisis came in 2006, with a spark that flew from an unexpected flame. In July, the government signed the Darfur Peace Agreement (DPA) with the Minnawi faction of the SLA, a Zaghawa group that

....

[123] Interview with human rights activist, name and place withheld, April 2010.

had mobilized among Zaghawa drought migrants in the area. Zaghawa soldiers of the SLA, who were now allies of the government, demanded the disarmament of the Habbaniya private militias, claiming that they were responsible for security. The Habbaniya private militias made an alliance with Fellata private militias and attacked the Zaghawa areas of the Goz Dango and Gereida, further to the east. It was an exceptionally brutal set of attacks—there were several reports of small children being thrown into burning huts—and these attacks displaced nearly all the goz farmers to the urban periphery in Nyala, where many now live.[124] The policy of ethnicizing relationships in South Darfur had ended the successful agricultural experiment of the Goz Dango for good.

Some of the farmers of the Goz Dango fled south instead. About 4,000 went to Boro Medina, and others to Timsah. Many of these people are now internally displaced northerners in Southern Sudan. A representative of these groups listed their ethnic origins in a 2010 interview: 'Bornu, Hottia, Kara, Zaghawa, Maliya, Misseriya Jebel, Masalit, Birgidd.' Most of these people were drought migrants, following routes similar to those followed by Fertit groups after the fall of the Fur sultanate in 1916. They were not, however, going to an ungoverned space, but to an IDP camp organized under GoSS authority, in a highly-militarized border zone of Sudan.

Fighting between Kara and Binga groups in 2006

The ethnicization of politics in South Darfur affected relations between some of the groups who had moved to the Goz Dango, including Zaghawa pastoralists who were using the rich lands of the area as a means to shift to a sedentary life. Most of these pastoralists lived in settlements to the west of Wadi Ibra, a seasonal watercourse that marked the eastern border of the goz. The southern border of the goz is the Umbelacha River, where many of the people who fled the burning of Kafia Kingi in 1930

---

124 OHCHR and UNMIS (2006); internal UN reports for the period.

lived: some of them were still there 70 years later. In the 1930s, all these Kafia Kingi refugees came under one umda, and successive umdas were chosen from different tribes. But in the 1970s and 1980s, people's views of ethnicity became more emphatic, and these views were expressed through demands for the creation of new umudiyas for specific groups. Dissensions between Kara and Binga groups emerged in the 1990s, with each group wanting its own umda. The Habbaniya nazir, responsible for tribal appointments, agreed to two new umudiyas.

Outsiders still often classify Binga and Kara people together as a group. But tensions between them continued. Binga people promoted the idea that Kara people were from CAR, and claimed that Kafia Kingi was their *hakura*, using a term for a tribal estate granted by the Fur sultans.[125] After the Darfur civil war started, these differing accounts of historical origins acquired new urgency, and they began to be enmeshed in national politics. At the time, both Kara and Binga people held posts in the ruling NCP. But in 2004, some rebel movements tried to organize in the villages along the Umbelacha where Kara and Binga people lived.

Young Kara men in Deim Bishara joined the SLA, and Binga people asked the governor for weapons, to fight them. Fighting lasted from August to December, and ended after a government-sponsored reconciliation conference (see Figure 7 above). The fighting displaced an enormous number of people, many of them fleeing to Boro Medina, just south of the Kafia Kingi enclave. In 2008, over 600 of these refugees moved to Minamba, the Kara and Binga village that the British had set up in 1930 (in 2006, there were only 187 Kara inhabitants in Minamba, so the arrival of Darfurian refugees transformed the place). Kara and Binga children attend the same school in Minamba. Commenting on ethnic tensions, Kara people in Minamba said:

> The Darfur problems between Kara and Binga do not affect
> Kara relations in Southern Sudan. The politics of strife

....

[125] Interview with Radom resident, name withheld, May 2010.

has entered Darfur. We are still intermarrying [with Binga people].[126]

The borderlands after the CPA

The signing of the CPA did not bring peace to the borderlands between Southern Sudan and Darfur. Instead, the war in Darfur generated new cultural borders between groups perceived as Arabs or non-Arabs. People who had been divided or displaced by British Southern Policy in 1930 found themselves negotiating violently reconfigured ethnic relationships in the area, and thousands of them were displaced to or within Darfur. The fighting in Darfur also provoked the first major displacement from Darfur to Southern Sudan since the fall of the Fur sultanate in 1916. The people of Goz Dango and Raga county shared the experience of crisis and neglect that is a feature of peripheral societies, but their crises unfolded in different ways, and at different tempos.

The violence in Darfur is entangled with its modernization: many Goz Dango farmers were children of pastoralists; now they are urban shanty-dwellers, trying to make a living in the IDP camps of Nyala. IDP camps have also been set up in Boro Medina. In Minamba, however, Kara people displaced from the Umbelacha River have made an unexpected return to a home chosen for them by British colonialists many decades ago. Now, after dealing with two wars, they and the other inhabitants of the borderlands have a new challenge: the effects of a likely new international border between Darfur and Southern Sudan.

....

[126] Interview with Kara people in Minamba, March 2010.

11. Conclusion: the Kafia Kingi enclave on the eve of the referendum

This report has presented a history of interlinked societies in Kafia Kingi and in adjacent areas to the north and south. The aim has been to analyse the sources of identity of the inhabitants of this remote Sudanese border-land, and their relation to the state, to their trades, livelihoods and labour systems, to the natural environment, and to the wars that have shaped their histories.

Fertit as Sudanese

'Fertit', the collective term for the inhabitants of this part of western Sudan, formerly pejorative, has undergone a striking evolution in contemporary Sudan, as illustrated in the following examples of its current range of meaning:

> When I was young I considered myself Belanda. It has become important now, to differ between non-Dinka. Even in Juba now the non-Dinka are called Fertit. *A Belanda chief.*

> It's pejorative. Originally Dinka people used it in a pejorative way. Now the Fertit are using it to rob the oppressor of his linguistic tools. *A Southern Sudanese academic.*

> A considerable portion of the north–south border runs through Hajj Yusuf [a Khartoum neighbourhood with a very diverse population]. In Sudanese universities people call themselves Fertit, it's a rehabilitated term. Dinka people

> married to Greeks, Fur, Arabs, they use the term. *A Khartoum
> journalist.*

The histories of hybridity, subordination and migration invoked here are not unusual in Sudan. In fact variations on such experiences can be seen as a central part of the lives of many Sudanese. The current use of the term 'Fertit' as a self-description by people in Khartoum who have no links to Western Bahr al-Ghazal is a striking expansion of its meaning to include a wider range of contemporary Sudanese people. In the early twentieth century, it may be noted, the term *sudani*, Sudanese, was also initially pejorative and used in a similar way to describe those people who had emerged into a new form of national consciousness from the experiences of war, slavery, urbanization and military life.

The migrations and upheavals of the last two centuries have scattered Fertit people across Sudan and made many of them into city dwellers. This, too, is an experience shared by many people in Sudan today—including Darfurian migrants in Southern Sudan. Fertit people now live throughout the country in archipelagos made up of urban clubs, rural traditional authorities and long-distance marriages. Sudan's urbanization rate is one of the fastest in Africa, the outcome of a history that has exposed many of the communities within its borders to pressures from faraway markets, and a political system that has created a particularly stark difference between its centre and its periphery. The social and cultural groups described in his report—such as the Kara club in Omdurman, or the Binga Association—are examples of the means whereby Sudanese people of these—and many other—ethnic groups deal with urbanization and the dislocations of a harsh economic system. Similar organizations for Darfurians exist in both northern and Southern Sudanese cities.

A succession of governments at the centre have helped to create these archipelagos through policies that make migration unavoidable. At times, they have tried to prevent migrants organizing around ethnicity, but today, in ethnic associations, the NCP and the SPLM both find malleable partners who can strike political deals on behalf of ethnic constituencies. The 2010 elections showed that Sudan's two ruling parties each have near total control over their respective spheres: almost everyone in the south voted for the SPLM, and almost everyone in the north voted for the NCP. It is within this new party structure that associations linking city migrants to rural Sudan, often based on ethnicity, will continue to play a part in shaping identities and the connections between the state and identity-based political communities.

Labour and livelihoods

The economies of Kafia Kingi and Raga have been drawn into Sudanese and international markets during the twentieth century. The development of these and other peripheral areas in Sudan has been an extremely violent process. The wars of the past few decades are entangled with government policies that cut off investment in the periphery and forced people there to improvise new and sometimes harsh means to earn a livelihood. Much of the economic infrastructure of these areas was built up during wartime, some of it by war itself, or other kinds of coercion.

The construction of roads, seen as a sine qua non of development, is not always beneficent. In the case of Raga and Kafia Kingi, although cross-border road building could contribute to peaceful trade and human movement, it should not be assumed that economic development of the area will be the automatic result. Roads can be a means of state control and increased militarization. Raga's roads have also contributed to human displacement. Many of the descendents of the forest peoples of nineteenth-century Bahr al-Ghazal have now moved to towns. This is the outcome of long historical processes that are pulling people from peripheral areas to urban centres.

In South Darfur, the route to urbanization has been even more rapid (Flint, 2010, p. 45). Until 2006, Goz Dango, on the borderlands of South Darfur, was the site of a social experiment on the part of some Darfuris seeking to adapt their livelihoods to climate change. Pastoralists moving from the arid north successfully built up an agricultural economy there. But this was destroyed in one of the many cruel sub-conflicts triggered by the war in Darfur. Many of these migrants have now been urbanized, and live in the IDP camps or shanty towns on the outskirts of Nyala.

Others have moved to towns in Western Bahr al-Ghazal.

Pastoralists from South Darfur—most of them Baggara—also appear to be making a turn towards farming, sometimes moving to the lands around Timsah, just east of the Kafia Kingi enclave, where they are involved in seasonal cultivation. These developments are occurring at a time of extremely rapid growth in livestock numbers among pastoralists across Sudan's north–south borderlands, and deterioration in the quality of rangelands (UNEP, 2007, pp. 186ff; World Bank, 2009, p. 80). In the years after 2006, disputes over access to pasture have been implicated in many local conflicts in Darfur. This is partly due to the fact that many farmers had been displaced to towns by 2006; subsequent conflicts often took place between newly militarized pastoralist groups who had formerly been allies with the government. They appear also to be behind an unexpected explosion of violence in Balbala, just north of Timsah, in April 2010, when more than a hundred Rizeigat cattle-keepers were killed in a fight with the SPLA.

The natural environment of the borderlands

A common feature of the inhabitants of the borderlands around the Kafia Kingi enclave—whether they are established farmers or drought migrants from North Darfur—is that they are all engaged in adapting to climate change. The enclave itself is a nature reserve, recognized as a UNESCO Biosphere Reserve, an international reservation that commits national government to sustainable development for the local population. But this is not a policy that has been actively pursued by government authorities: instead, people in the far-western villages of the enclave have been displaced by a decision to extend the reserved area in the 1990s. The reservation does not seem to have protected many mammalian species, which have seen a dramatic decline linked to the desperate livelihood strategies of local populations over the past few decades. The northern and Southern wildlife services in Bahr al-Ghazal and Darfur are administratively separated and are not in communication with each other, and so little has been done to halt this decline.

The copper mine at Hofrat al-Nahas and other mineral wealth of the area are at the centre of political calculations about its future—even though there have been few profits made from the enclave's minerals in the past 90 years. Alternative economic futures for the area have hardly begun to be discussed.

Border wars

Since the 1960s, political forces outside the centre of power in Sudan have intermittently sought a structure capable of mobilizing the disaffections of both Darfur and the south, but this goad has remained elusive. Southern nationalists hoped for support from Darfur in the early 1960s. One of the first southern nationalist groups, the Sudan African Closed Districts Union, kept seats on its executive committee vacant in the hope that Fur and other marginalized northern people would fill them (Malok, 2009, p. 44). None did. This period saw the emergence of regionalist sentiment in Darfur, with organizations such as the Darfur Development Front, and its unsuccessful military wing Suni, bringing together Baggara, Fur and other Darfurian groups.[127] A Suni statement from 1966 invoked southern struggles:

> O people of Kordofan, the Nubia Mountains, the Darfur,
> the Suni Organization appeals to you to unite against the
> Norther[n] bloodsucking imperialism which has sucked your
> blood in the name of religion... the northern imperialists who
> have killed your brothers in the south... murdering nearly two
> million (NA/FO371/190419).

Suni members were rounded up before they could fire a shot and the Darfur Development Front was incorporated into Khartoum politics. A few years later, the Anyanya rebellion in Southern Sudan concluded with the 1972 Addis Ababa peace deal, which established autonomous political

---

[127] Interview with Yusuf Takana, former federal minister of international cooperation and former Darfur commissioner, Khartoum, May 2010.

structures for the south, setting people seeking change in Darfur and Southern Sudan on different tracks.

The possibility still exists for the distinct but interlinked conflicts in Darfur and Southern Sudan to enmesh with each other. This happened in the 1870s, when an army from Bahr al-Ghazal overthrew the sultanate in Darfur, and it almost happened again in 1991, when Daud Bolad, a Darfurian Islamist, joined the SPLA and attempted an invasion through Kafia Kingi. The possibility exists not only in the Kafia Kingi enclave but also in the Rizeigat lands further east, which have witnessed both conflicts with and defections to the SPLA in the past six years. Meanwhile, the rumours of LRA activity in the area may well be just rumours, but they are an indication of the complexity of the situation, and leave open the possibility of Ugandan involvement in the area.

Future conflict in the area is thus a distinct possibility, but war is not inevitable. There are structural reasons for the two most heavily armed groups in Sudan—the SAF and the SPLA—to maintain the current ceasefire, which lie in the economic interdependence of governments in Juba and Khartoum. Reworking identities, economies and ecologies of this remote periphery are ways to help consolidate the current peace.

12. Recommendations

The fate of the peoples of the Kafia Kingi enclave and the wider area of Raga and Radom has historically been obscured by larger-scale social and political struggles taking place in Sudan. Today, in the light of the negotiations over the country's political future and the demarcation of the north–south border, the area and its people have acquired a new diplomatic importance. The current level of international attention and the extent of the international presence in Sudan make it possible for the interests of this neglected sector of the population to be reflected in the search for country-level solutions. The future of the Kafia Kingi enclave in particular will be a critical element in post-referendum negotiations between the two parties to the CPA.

In negotiations over post-referendum arrangements in Sudan between the two parties to the CPA, there should be explicit consideration of the future administration of the Kafia Kingi enclave and the implications for the wider area of Raga and Radom.

Despite its importance in the negotiations over the north–south border under the terms of the CPA, the area itself has remained inaccessible to both the UN missions in Sudan. Neither UNAMID (in Darfur) nor UNMIS (in southern Sudan and the north–south border areas) has been permitted to move in Kafia Kingi or its environs, so there is little information on the current situation there. Access to this highly militarized area is crucial if a peaceful transition is to be achieved by the end of the interim period laid down in the CPA.

External monitoring during the remainder of the CPA period is vital to the future of the north–south border areas. The UN should press the

two parties to the CPA to allow immediate access to the Kafia Kingi enclave and its environs in anticipation of post-referendum negotiations on future administrative arrangements.

A future administration of Kafia Kingi, established after post-referendum negotiations are concluded, will have the opportunity to establish a model administration, one that respects the rights of the people of the enclave and provides a basis for the future economic development of the area. Administrative arrangements for the enclave need to respect its ambiguous position vis-à-vis the divide between north and south in Sudan. Freedom of movement, soft borders, access to land and free trade will help safeguard livelihoods in the area. Meetings between state governments and between neighbouring communities in the borderlands could help maintain peace, as they have done in the past.

International support should be offered for the development of an administrative plan for the future of the Kafia Kingi enclave, including consultations with representatives of the communities that live in and around it and consideration of future relations between the state governments of Western Bahr al-Ghazal and South Darfur.

The mineral wealth of Kafia Kingi has been at the centre of political calculations about the future of the enclave, yet despite a century of exploitation yields from mining have been minimal. The area's resources of timber and wildlife merit as much attention as its mineral resources. Future economic development could include sustainable forestry, tourism and the international market for carbon emissions (discussed inconclusively by the Federal Ministry of Agriculture in 2009).

Support for economic development in Kafia Kingi from government authorities and aid-givers should include planning for sustainable exploitation of its natural resources and environmental management of development projects. The latter should be subject to a regime of conservation that covers minerals, water resources, forestry and wildlife.

The history of Kafia Kingi and the wider area around it, including Raga and Radom, means that its inhabitants defy easy categorization as northerners, southerners or westerners. This diversity is a cultural resource, a contribution to Sudanese national identity, and should be reflected in education at local and national level.

Schools, universities and cultural and historical organizations in the border states should be supported to pursue research and education into the cultural heritage of the western borderlands including academic exchanges between institutions in South Darfur and Western Bahr al-Ghazal and collaboration with international NGOs and research organizations.

References

Abd al-Azim, Shawqi (2010) *kafi kinji aw hufrat al-nahhas: shararat al-harb al-thalitha* [Kafia Kingi or Hofrat al-Nahas, the spark of the third war]. 22 August. al-Akhbar: Khartoum.

Abdalla, Abdalla Ahmed (2006) 'Environmental degradation and conflict in Darfur: experiences and development options.' In Bakri Saeed (ed.) *Environmental Degradation as a Cause of Conflict in Darfur*. University for Peace: Addis Ababa.

Abdel Rahim, Muddathir (1966) 'The development of British policy in the Southern Sudan 1899–1947.' *Middle Eastern Studies*, Vol. 2, No. 3, pp. 227–49.

Adams, Martin (1982) 'The Baggara problem: attempts at modern change in Southern Darfur and Southern Kordofan (Sudan).' *Development and Change*, Vol. 13, No. 2, pp. 259–89.

African Development Bank (1998) *Sudan: Country Strategy Paper, 1998–2001*. Abidjan.

al-Hasan, Musa al-Mubarak (1995) *tarikh dar fur al-siyasi* [Political history of Darfur]. dar al-khartum lil-tiba wa-l-nashr wa-l-tawzi: Khartoum.

Alier, Abel (2003) *Southern Sudan: Too Many Agreements Dishonoured*. Abel Alier: Khartoum.

Aliyu, Muhammad Isa (2008) *al-alaqat bayn al-rizayqat wa-dinka malwal* [Relations between the Rizeigat and the Dinka Malual]. Thesis. Omdurman Islamic University: Omdurman.

al-Tunisi, Muhammad Umar (nd) *tashhidh al-adhhan bi-sirat bilad al-arab wa-l-sudan* [A whetting of the minds, in the story of the land of the Arabs and Sudan]. al-muasisa al-misriya al-ama li-l-talif wa-l-anba wa-l-nashr: Cairo.

Badal, Raphael K. (1986) 'Oil and regional sentiment in the South.' In Muddathir Abd Al-Rahim, et al. (eds.) *Sudan Since Independence: Studies of the Political Development since 1956*. Gower: Aldershot.

—— (1994) 'Political cleavages within Southern Sudan: an empirical analysis of the re-division debate.' In Sharif Harir and Terje Tvedt (eds.) *Short-Cut to Decay: the Case of the Sudan*. Nordiska Afrikainstitutet: Uppsala.

Baer, Gabriel (1969) 'Slavery and its abolition.' In Gabriel Baer (ed.) *Studies in the Social History of Modern Egypt*. University of Chicago Press: Chicago, IL.

Balamoun, G. Ayoub (1981) *Peoples and Economics in the Sudan 1884–1956: The First Part of a History of Human Tragedies on the Nile (1884–1984)*. Harvard University Center for Population Studies: Cambridge, MA.

Beshir, Mohamed Omer (1968) *The Southern Sudan: Background to Conflict*. Hurst: London.

B.G.P. 16.B.2, 'Administration of Districts: Western District, Bahr El Ghazal Province,' in folder marked Civil Sec A/1 vol. 1, Districts Reorganisation, Western District, Wau archives, unclassified.

B.G.P./SCR/8-A-3, 'Letter from Ingleson, Governor Bahr el-Ghazal to Civil Secretary, Wau 10 Jan 35. The Western District.' Andrew Baring papers, unclassified.

B.G.P./SCR/I.C.6, 'Administrative policy, Southern Provinces', 22 March 1930, Bahr al-Ghazal province governor Brock to Civil Secretary, reproduced in the collection British Southern Policy in the Sudan (nd).

Billiton PLC (1999) *Annual Report*. Billiton PLC: London

Center for Disease Control (1995) 'Implementation of health initiatives during a cease-fire—Sudan, 1995.' *MMWR Weekly*, Vol. 44, No. 23, pp. 433–36. <http://www.cdc.gov/mmwr/preview/mmwrhtml/00038071.htm>

Chinyankandath, James (1991) 'The 1986 elections.' In Peter Woodward (ed.) *Sudan After Nimeiri*. London: Routledge.

Clarence-Smith, William G. (2008) 'Islamic abolitionism in the Western Indian Ocean from c. 1800.' Paper given at a conference entitled *Slavery and the Slave Trades in the Indian Ocean and Arab Worlds: Global Connections and Disconnections* at Yale University, USA.

Collins, Robert O. (1983) *Shadows in the Grass: Britain in the Southern Sudan, 1918–1956*. Yale University Press: New Haven, CT.

Committee for the Redivision of the Southern Provinces (nd, approximately 1975). *Final Report*.

Comyn, D.C.E. (1911) *Service and Sport in the Sudan: A Record of Administration in the Anglo-Egyptian Sudan. With Some Intervals of Sport and Travel*. John Lane, The Bodley Head: London.

Cordell, Dennis D. (1985) *Dar al-Kuti and the Last Years of the Trans-Saharan Slave Trade*. University of Wisconsin Press: Madison, WI.

CS/16-B.1/4, 'Note,' R.K.W, Civil Secretary's Office, 20 November 1930, Wau archives, unclassified.

de Waal, Alex (1989) *Famine that Kills: Darfur 1984–1985*. Clarendon Press: Oxford.

de Waal, Alex, and A.H. Abdel Salam (2004) 'Islamism, state power and *jihad* in Sudan.' In Alex de Waal (ed.) *Islamism and its Enemies in the Horn of Africa*. Hurst: London.

Democratic Republic of the Sudan (1983) *Population of the Sudan and its Regions, Project Documentation No 2, 1983 Census, Total Populations by Male, Female & Sex Ratio for Region, Province & District*. Population Studies Centre, University of Gezira: Gezira.

DR.P/66-B-45, 'The Munro–Wheatley Agreement. Rizeigat–Dinka (Malwal), Safaha,' 22 April 1924, Andrew Baring papers, unclassified.

DP.R SCR 66-B-44 vol. 1, 'Notes on Kafia Kingi Area. (Starting 1924)' (nd), Andrew Baring papers, unclassified. The note reviews discussions about the area's borders from 1924 to 1946, with file references.

Elbashier, Abdul Aziz Ahmed (2010) *A Word from the Chairman*. EYAT Oilfield Services website. <http://www.eyatoil.com/About.html>

El Shibly, Mekki Medani (1990) *Fiscal Federalism in Sudan*. Khartoum University Press: Khartoum

Evans-Pritchard, E.E. (1963) 'The Zande State.' *Journal of the Royal Anthropological Institute of Great Britain and Ireland*, Vol. 93, No. 1, pp. 134–54.

—— (1971) *The Azande: History and Political Institutions*. Clarendon: Oxford.

Ewald, Janet J. (1990) *Soldiers, Traders and Slaves: State Formation and Economic Transformation in the Greater Nile Valley, 1700–1885*. University of Wisconsin Press: Madison, WI.

Fadul, Abduljabbar Abdalla (2006) 'Natural resources management for sustainable peace in Darfur.' In Bakri Saeed (ed.) *Environmental Degradation as a Cause of Conflict in Darfur*. University for Peace: Addis Ababa.

Fula Boki Tombe Gale, Severino (2002) *Shaping a Free Southern Sudan: Memoirs of our Struggle 1934–1985*. Loa Catholic Missions Council: Loa.

Garang, Joseph (1971) *The Dilemma of the Southern Intellectual*. Ministry of Southern Affairs: Khartoum.

Gessi, Romolo (1892) *Seven Years in the Soudan*. Sampson, Low, Marston: London.

Gide, André (1927) *Voyage au Congo*. Gallimard: Paris.

Gray, Richard (1961) *A History of the Southern Sudan, 1839–1889*. Oxford University Press: Oxford.

GoS (Government of Sudan) (2008) 'Memorial of the Government of Sudan.' In *Permanent Court of Arbitration* [The Hague]. *In the matter of an arbitration before a tribunal constituted in accordance with Article 5 of the Arbitration Agreement between the Government of Sudan and the Sudan People's Liberation Movement/Army on delimiting Abyei Area*. 18 December. GoS: Khartoum.

GoS and Eastern Front (2006) *Eastern Sudan Peace Agreement*. Asmara.

GoS and SPLM (Sudan People's Liberation Movement) (2005) *Comprehensive Peace Agreement*. Naivasha.

GoS et al. (1972) *Addis Ababa Agreement*. Khartoum. Signed by GoS and various southern rebel groups.

GoS et al. (1997) *Khartoum Peace Agreement*. Khartoum. Signed by GoS and various southern rebel groups.

GoS et al. (2006) *Darfur Peace Agreement*. Abuja. Signed by GoS and various Darfur rebel groups.

GoSS (Government of Southern Sudan) (2005) *Interim Constitution of Southern Sudan*. Juba.

Hargey, Taj (1999) 'Festina lente: slavery policy and practice in the Anglo-Egyptian Sudan.' In Suzanne Miers and Martin A. Klien (eds.) *Slavery and Colonial Rule in Africa*. Cass: London.

Hassan, Tarig Tag Elsir, et al. (2005) *Sustainable Utilization of Wildlife Resources in Radom Biosphere Reserve (Final Report)*. <http://www.unesco.org/mab/doc/mys/2001/sudan.pdf>

Herbert, G.K.C. (1926) 'The Bandala of the Bahr el Ghazal'. *Sudan Notes and Records*, Vol. 8, pp. 187–94.

Hill, Richard (1951) *A Bibliographical Dictionary of the Anglo-Egyptian Sudan*. Clarendon: Oxford.

Holt, P. (1970) *The Mahdist State in the Sudan, 1881–1898: A Study of its Origins, Development and Overthrow*. Clarendon: Oxford.

Human Rights Watch (1999) *Famine in Sudan: The Human Rights Causes*. Human Rights Watch: New York, NY.

Hunting Technical Services (1974) *Southern Darfur Land-Use Planning Survey*. Ministry of Agriculture, Food and Natural Resources: Khartoum, and Hunting Technical Services: Borehamwood.

Ibrahim, Ahmad Muhammad Ahmad (2008) *tasfiyat al-idara al-ahliya wa-nataijuha fi dar fur* [The Abolition of Native Administration and its Consequences in Dar Fur]. sharikat matabi al-sudan li-l-umla al-mahduda: Khartoum.

International Criminal Court (2007) 'Situation in Darfur, The Sudan (Public Redacted Version): Prosecutor's application under Article 58(7).' ICC-02/05, 27 February. International Criminal Court: The Hague.

Jackson, H.C. (1913) *Black Ivory and White, or The Story of El Zubeir Pasha Slaver and Sultan as Told by Himself.* Blackwell: Oxford.

Johnson, Douglas H. (2007) *The Root Causes of Sudan's Civil Wars.* James Currey: Oxford.

—— (2010) *When Boundaries Become Borders: The Impact of Boundary Making on Southern Sudan's Border Zones.* Rift Valley Institute: London and Nairobi.

Jok, Jok Madut (2001) *War and Slavery in Sudan.* University of Pennsylvania Press: Philadelphia, PA.

Kalck, Pierre (2005) *Historical Dictionary of the Central African Republic.* Scarecrow: Lanham, MD.

Klugman, Jeni, and Asbjorn Wee (2007) *Darfur: Dimensions of Challenge for Development: A Background Volume.* World Bank: Washington, DC.

Lewis, M.P. (ed.) (2009) *Ethnologue: Languages of the World.* (Sixteenth edition.) SIL International: Dallas, TX.

MacMichael, H.A. (1922) *A History of the Arabs in the Sudan, and Some Account of the People who Preceded them and of the Tribes Inhabiting Darfur.* Cambridge University Press: Cambridge.

Mahmud, Adil Abd al-Rahman (2006) *qabail al-baqqara fi gharb al-sudan: bahth fi usulihim wa-ansabihim wa-thaqafatihim* [The Baqqara Tribes in the West of Sudan: A Study of their Origins, Lineage and Culture]. al-Alamiya: Sudan.

Ministry of Finance and Economic Planning (2008) *Supplementary Budget.* Government of Southern Sudan: Juba.

Mire, Lawrence (1986) 'Al-Zubayr Pasha and the Zariba Based Slave Trade in the Bahr al-Ghazal 1855–1879.' In John Ralph Willis (ed.) *Slaves and Slavery in Muslim Africa: The Servile Estate.* Routledge: London.

Mohamed, Hamid Mannan, El-Fatih Idris A. Karim and Mohamed Ibrahim Mohamed (1998) 'Hashish cultivation in the state of Southern Darfour, Sudan.' *Eastern Mediterranean Health Journal*, Vol. 4, No. 1, pp. 114–21.

Morton, James (2005) *A Darfur Compendium: A Review of the Geographical, Historical and Economic Background to Development in the Region.* HTSPE: Hemel Hempstead.

Muhammad, Farah Isa (1982) *al-turath al-shabi li-qabilat al-ta aysha* [Popular heritage of the Taysha tribe]. shubat al-fulklur, mahad al-dirasat al-ifriqiya wa-l-asyawiya. Khartoum University Press: Khartoum.

NA/FO/10/776, Correspondence between the chairman of the Anglo-Belgian African Company Ltd and British Tropical Africa Company Ltd, and the Under-Secretary for Foreign Affairs (1902). NA (National Archive, London)

NA/FO371/190419, Text of SUNI communiqué in British embassy note on political parties, 6 April 1966.

NA/WO/106/14, 'Letter from Wingate to Ali Dinar'.

NA/OD/20/524, 'South Darfur rural development project paper,' April 1975

ND/SCR/1/C/1, Undated letter to Governor, Bahr al-Ghazal Province, reproduced in the collection *British Southern Policy in the Sudan* (nd).

No. 66 A 20/21, Letter from District Commissioner, Western District to Governor, Equatoria, 9 August 1939, in Wau archive file, unclassified, entitled *Runaways Story with its Deplorable Ending.*

Nyaba, Peter Adwok (2000) *Politics of Liberation in South Sudan: An Insider's View.* Fountain: Kampala.

O'Fahey, R.S. (1980) *State and Society in Dar Fur.* Hurst: London.

—— (1982) 'Fur and Fartit: the history of a frontier.' In John Mack and Peter Robertshaw (eds.) *Culture History in the Southern Sudan: Archaeology, Linguistics, Ethnohistory.* British Institute in Eastern Africa: Nairobi.

OHCHR (Office of the High Commissioner for Human Rights) and UNMIS (United Nations Mission in the Sudan) (2006) 'Killings of civilians by militia in Buram Locality, South Darfur, 6 October 2006.' *Fifth periodic report of the United Nations High Commissioner for Human Rights on the situation of human rights in the Sudan.* OHCHR: Geneva.

Parry, D.E., and G.E. Wickens (1981) 'The Qozes of Southern Darfur Sudan Republic,' *Geographical Journal*, Vol. 147, No. 3, pp. 307–320.

Paysama, Stanislaus Abdullahi (nd) *How a Slave Became a Minister: Autobiography of Sayyed Stanislaus Abdullahi Paysama.* Photocopied book from the library of Yusuf Takana. No publishing details available.

Presidency of the Republic (2009) *mashru dirasat tanmiyat al-ruhal wa-l-mujtamat al-mustaqirra bi-hawd bahr al-arab, wilayat janub dar fur* [Project for the development of nomads and settled societies in the Bahr al-Arab basin]. South Darfur State: Khartoum.

Reining, Conad C. (1966) *The Zande Scheme: An Anthropological Case Study of Development in Africa*. Northwestern University Press: Evanston, IL.

Republic of Sudan (1957) *First Population Census of Sudan, 1955/6, Fourth Interim Report*. Ministry of Social Affairs: Khartoum.

—— (1960) 'Description of revised boundary between Bahr El Ghazal and Darfur Provinces.' *Sudan Government Gazette* 947, 15 June.

République centrafricaine (1978) *Annuaire Statistique*. République centrafricaine: Bangui.

—— (1989) *Annuaire Statistique*. Direction de la Statistique Générale et des Etudes Economiques: Bangui.

Roden, David (1974) 'Regional inequality and rebellion in the Sudan.' *Geographical Review*. Vol. 64, No. 4, pp. 498–516.

SAD/529/1, 'Raga Sub-District', Robertson papers. SAD (Sudan Archive, Durham) (NB For in-text citations, extra numbers following the code indicate page numbers.)

SAD/542/18, E.S. Jackson (1910/11) *Report on Southern District of Bahr el Ghazal*.

SAD/710, *Western District Annual Report*, (1939).

SAD/735/4, G.D. Lampen, *The Baqqara Tribes of Darfur*, notebook.

SAD/815/7, *Western District Bahr el-Ghazal Province Handbook* (1954).

Santandrea, Stefano (1953) 'A preliminary account of the Indri, Togoyo, Feroge, Mangaya and Woro.' *Sudan Notes and Records*. Vol. 34, Part 2, pp. 230–64.

—— (1955) 'The Belgians in Western Bahr el Ghazal.' *Sudan Notes and Records*. Vol. 36, Part 2, p. 188.

—— (1964) *A Tribal History of the Western Bahr El Ghazal*. Editrice Nigrizia: Bologna.

—— (1980) 'Ndogo ethonological texts (Sudan): with translation and commentary.' *Anthropos*, Vol. 75, pp. 823–904.

—— (1981) *Ethno-Geography of the Bahr El Ghazal (Sudan)*. Editrice Missionaria Italiana: Bologna.

—— (nd) *The Banda of the Bahr El Ghazal (Sudan): short ethnological notes*. Pro manuscripto.

Scott, James C. (2009) *The Art of Not Being Governed: An Anarchist History of Upland South East Asia*. Yale University Press: New Haven, CI.

SDD/SCR/66-D-3, Memo to Governor Darfur from District Commissioner South Darfur, 23 Apr 1933, 'Note on the Settlement of Awlad Arab,' Andrew Baring papers, unclassified.

Seekers of Truth and Justice (2004) *The Black Book: Imbalance of Power and Wealth in Sudan*. English translation of a book attributed to the Justice and Equality Movement. No publishing details available.

Sikainga, Ahmad A. (1983) *The Western Bahr al-Ghazal under British Rule*. Ohio University Press: Athens, OH.

Southern Sudan Centre for Census, Statistics and Evaluation (2009) *Statistical Yearbook for Southern Sudan, 2009*. Southern Sudan Centre for Census, Statistics and Evaluation: Juba.

Southern Development Investigation Team (1955) *Natural Resources and Development Potential in the Southern Provinces of the Sudan*. Sudan Government: London.

Sudan Radio Service (2010) 'South Darfur Governor dismisses claims of LRA presence in state.' Sudan Radio Service: Nairobi. 20 October. <http://www.sudanradio.org/south-darfur-governor-dismisses-claims-lra-presence-state>

Sudan Transition and Recovery Database (2003) *Report on Raga Area*. Office of the UN Resident and Humanitarian Coordinator for the Sudan: Nairobi.

Suret-Canale, Jean (1971) *French Colonialism in Tropical Africa, 1900–1945*. Pica: New York, NY.

Takana, Yusuf (2008) *The Politics of Regional Boundaries and Conflict in Sudan: the South Darfur Case*. Sudan Working Paper No. 2. Chr. Michelsen Institute: Bergen.

Theobald, A.B. (1965) *Ali Dinar, Last Sultan of Darfur, 1898–1916*. Longmans, Green: London.

Thomas, Edward (2010) *Decisions and Deadlines: A Critical Year for Sudan*, Chatham House: London.

—— (2009) *Against the Gathering Storm: Securing Sudan's Comprehensive Peace Agreement*. Chatham House: London.

Tubiana, Jérôme (2009) 'Learning from Darfur.' *Dispatches: Out of Poverty*, No. 4.

Tucker, A.N. (1931) 'The tribal confusion around Wau.' *Sudan Notes and Records*, Vol. 14, pp. 49–60.

Tucker, A.N., and M.A. Bryan (1966) *Linguistic Analyses: The Non-Bantu Languages of North-Eastern Africa*. London/Oxford: International African Institute/Oxford University Press.

UNDP (United Nations Development Programme) (1973) *Mineral Survey in Three Selected Areas, Sudan. Technical Report 4, Copper Exploration in the Hofrat En Nahas Area, Western Sudan, an Interim Report*. United Nations: New York, NY.

UNESCO (United Nations Educational, Scientific and Cultural Organization) (2007) *Biosphere Reserve Information*. The MAB Programme. <http://www.unesco.org/mabdb/br/brdir/directory/biores.asp?mode=all&code=SUD+02>

Vezzadini, Elena (2008) *The 1924 Revolution: Hegemony, Resistance and Nationalism in the Colonial Sudan*. University of Bergen: Bergen.

Walsh, R.P.D. (1991) 'Climate, hydrology and water resources.' In G.M. Craig (ed.) *The Agriculture of the Sudan*. Oxford University Press: Oxford.

WD/66-A-20/24 (RAGA), response from Assistant District Commissioner B.J. Cocks, 20 September 1951, in Wau archive file, unclassified, entitled *The B + K Runaways Story with its Deplorable Ending*.

World Bank (2003) *Sudan Stabilization and Reconstruction: Country Economic Memorandum*. World Bank: Washington, DC.

—— (2009) *Sudan: The Road Towards Sustainable and Broad-Based Growth*. World Bank: Washington, DC.

Young, Helen, et al. (2005) *Darfur: Livelihoods Under Siege*. Feinstein International Famine Center, Tufts University: Medford, MA.

Zulfu, Ismat Hasan (1973) *Karari*. Maktabat al-Tawhid.

Glossary

Abbala	Arabic term for camel-keepers.
Aja	Small ethnic group with origin story in Boro Medina; forcibly moved to Kparakpara in 1930; now urbanized. Language similar to Kresh and Banda.
Anglo-Egyptian Sudan	Colonial regime, 1898–1955 (the British period); a Condominium, with Great Britain and Egypt theoretically ruling in partnership; in practice under British administration.
Anyanya	Army of the first post-independence armed rebellion in Southern Sudan, 1963–72.
Awlad Arab	Groups from different parts of West, Central and Sudanic Africa living in the Kafia Kingi enclave in the 1930s, perceived as Arabized or Islamized by British officials.
Baggara, Baqqara	Arabic term for cattle-keepers; in Sudan, the term refers to cattle-keeping and farming groups who live in savannah areas near the borders with Southern Sudan. Similar cattle-keeping groups exist on the southern fringe of the Sahara desert in other countries, where they are often called Arabs (for example, Chadian Arabs).
Banda	Group of tribes; most displaced by war from French Equatorial Africa to Bahr al-Ghazal after 1911; after 1930 settled at Sopo, south of Raga, also in CAR.
Bandala/ Mandala/ Ngbandala	Pejorative term for Arabic-speaking client groups formerly held in slavery by Rizeigat and sometimes other Baggara in South Darfur and Western Bahr al-Ghazal, each side of the north–south border, termed in this report Bahr al-Ghazal Rizeigat.
Bahr al-Ghazal	Tributary of the White Nile; also the name of a province that covered the western Nile Basin in south Sudan. (See note on the area under study.)
Bahr al-Ghazal Rizeigat	Term used in this paper to describe Bandala groups.

Belanda/ Belanda	Two larger ethnic groups, Belanda Boor or Bor; and Belanda Viri or Bviri. Bviri are speakers of a Ndogo language and their origin-stories link them to the sources of the Bussere and Namutina rivers, near the Congo watershed in the far south of Raga county. Boor speak an unrelated Luo language and have origin stories that connect them to the north east of Bahr al-Ghazal. The shared name probably comes from the time of Zande conquests.
Binga	Smaller group, with an origin story that links them to Jebel Marra in Darfur. Moved to what is now CAR and the Kafia Kingi enclave at the end of the Darfur sultanate; driven out by the colonial destruction of Kafia Kingi town in 1930. Some fled to Darfur to avoid forced settlement at Minamba, on the Raga road. Populations in Minamba, Darfur and across Sudan. Language similar to Kara and Yulu.
Bornu	Muslim state near Lake Chad, that was established in the eighth century and fell in 1894 to a Sudanese slavery entrepreneur; today the name of a Nigerian state. (Speakers of the Kanuri language of Bornu are spread across West and Central Africa, and, in Sudan, in Darfur and Bahr al-Ghazal.)
CAR	Central African Republic.
Commissioner	British commissioners were political officials responsible for a district, equivalent to a southern county or a northern locality today. In the early post-independence period, up to the 1970s and 1980s, a commissioner was responsible for a province (equivalent to a state governor today). From the 1990s to the present, a commissioner is the political officer responsible for a southern county or northern locality.
CPA	Comprehensive Peace Agreement, a 2005 deal that ended the civil war between the SPLM/A and the central government.
DPA	Darfur Peace Agreement, a 2006 deal signed by the Khartoum government and some of the many factions in the civil war in Darfur
DRC	Democratic Republic of the Congo, formerly Zaire.

Dar Abo Diima   South-western province of the Darfur sultanate in the late nineteenth century.

Dar Fertit/Fartit   'Fertit-land', name for the southern borderlands of Darfur; term sometimes extended to the non-Dinka and non-Luo areas of Western Bahr al-Ghazal.

Dar al-Kuti   Client state of the Sahelian sultanate of Wadai, transformed in the late nineteenth century into a slave-raiding state that devastated Central Africa. It was destroyed by a still-more devastating French conquest.

diya (diyya)   Term from Islamic law for payment of financial compensation for a criminal injury; in accepting it, the victim waives their right to demand a retributive punishment. Traditional authorities in many Sudanese tribes manage complex systems of compensation, and these systems help to give tribal structures legal form.

Erenga   Smaller group living on the Chad border and speaking a Nilo-Saharan language linked to Tama. Many moved south in the droughts of the 1970s and 1980s.

FEA   French Equatorial Africa, a federation of four French territories established in 1910 and lasting until 1960. Successor states are the Central African Republic, Chad, Gabon and Congo-Brazzaville.

Fellata/Fallata   Pastoralist, agrarian and urban speakers of Fulbe, (Fulani), a language of West African origin that is widely spoken in Sudan. The term is used to designate a wide variety of Sudanese of West African descent.

Feroghe/Feroge   Large ethnic group made up of speakers of Kaligi, with origin stories that link them to Darfur and its southern border, and a leading family descended from a Bornu hajj or Muslim pilgrim. Moved to Khor Shammam in the nineteenth and twentieth centuries; displaced to Raga in 1980s.

Fertit/Fartit   Catch-all word for non-Dinka, non-Arab, non-Luo, non-Fur groups of Western Bahr al-Ghazal; once a pejorative term, now with a complex range of meanings. See Chapter 4 for further discussion.

FFAMC	Fiscal and Financial Allocations Monitoring Commission, a body to ensure more central investment in the periphery, established by the CPA and invoked in other peace agreements.
Fur	Principal language and people group of Darfur, historically the occupants of the fertile uplands of Jebel Marra; they expanded southwards, incorporating other groups, a process that was accelerated by the establishment of the Fur sultanate in the seventeenth century.
Gbaya	See Kresh.
Gimir/Gimr/ Qimr	Group with origins in Kulbus, West Darfur, on the Chadian border; a minor sultanate from the 18th century, led by a sultan from the northern Nile valley. Pre-colonial travel literature indicates that they spoke a Nilo-Saharan language similar to Tama, but they are now Arabic speakers, and since the polarization of African and Arab identities in the civil war that began in 2003, some have identified as Arab. Many migrated to South Darfur during the droughts of the 1970s and 1980s, and in previous migrations.
GoSS	Government of Southern Sudan.
Governor	Under British rule, the chief political official of each of the nine provinces; in the 1970s and 1980s, the chief political official of each of the nine regions; and after 1994, the chief political official in each of 26 states (25 states after 2005).
goz	Stabilized sand dunes, a soil and water system that covers much of South Darfur.
Gula	Alternative name for Kara language.
Habbaniya	Arabic-speaking cattle-keepers (Baggara) whose traditional lands cover most of south-western Darfur (another Habbaniya group lives in Kordofan). Origin stories in Arabia or Tunisia; links with Fertit groups.
HEC	Higher Executive Council, the government of the semi-autonomous Southern Region of Sudan from 1973 to 1983.

Hofrat al-Nahas   Ancient mining settlement at northern edge of the Kafia Kingi enclave, currently under the administration of Radom locality in South Darfur state, formerly part of Bahr al-Ghazal. Hofrat al-Nahas means copper pit or copper mine in Arabic.

ICC   International Criminal Court, The Hague.

IDP   Internally displaced person.

Indiri   Smaller ethnic group with origin stories in Raga; when the British moved the Feroghe group to Raga, they came under the authority of the Feroghe chief until the end of the north–south civil war in 2005.

Ingaz (inqadh)   (National) Salvation. Name for the government formed after the coup in Sudan in 1989.

jallabiya   White, floor-length robe for men, usually perceived in Sudan as an Arab or Muslim style of dress.

JEM   Justice and Equality Movement, a Darfur rebel movement led by Khalil Ibrahim, a former member of the Ingaz regime's security forces. JEM is often linked to the Zaghawa ethnic group.

JIU   Joint Integrated Unit. Military units established by the CPA, combining troops from the SAF and SPLA.

Kafia Kingi enclave   Area of about 12,500 km2 towards the western end of the border between Darfur and Southern Sudan, sometimes referred to as Hofrat al-Nahas. The entire area is now part of the Radom Biosphere Reserve. (See also note on the area under study.)

Kaligi   Name for the ancestral core group of the Feroghe tribe and the language spoken by Feroghe people.

Kara (Gula)   Group with origin stories in Darfur and CAR, spread out across northern Sudan during the Mahdiya; moved to Kafia Kingi around the time of the fall of the Darfur sultanate in 1916. Forcibly settled in 1930 by the British in Minamba. Some fled to Darfur to avoid forced settlement. Language related to Binga and Yulu.

khalifa   Caliph, or successor: the title of the successors of the Sudanese Mahdi and the Prophet Muhammad.

khor   Seasonal watercourse.

KPA	Khartoum Peace Agreement, 1997, between the Government of Sudan and six southern parties and rebel movements.
Kresh/Kreish	Name for several groups with origin stories in Western Bahr al-Ghazal and present-day CAR. Some groups call themselves Gbaya, a name also claimed by other groups, such as Aja. Dongo people, with an origin story in Jebel Dango near Radom, are often classed as a separate ethnic group, but they speak the same language as Kresh people. Kresh Hofrat al-Nahas, also called Ngbongbo, take their name from the copper mines in the Kafia Kingi enclave. Uyujuku is the Kresh name for the town of Deim Zubeir: Kresh Ndogo (also called Gbaya Ndogo) people lived in the area and surrounding river valleys. In the British period, these different groups were moved to the road between Raga and Boro Medina. Some Kresh settlements on that road are now deserted; many Kresh people live in towns across Sudan.
kujur	Widespread pejorative Sudanese Arabic term used to refer to African traditional ritual specialists or their religious beliefs.
LRA	Lord's Resistance Army, Ugandan insurgent group, now active in DRC and CAR.
Mahdiya	The Mahdist revolution (1882–1885) and the Mahdist state (1885–1898).
Mangayat	Smaller ethnic group, with origin stories connecting them to the Mangayat hills south of Raga.
Masalit	Larger group living in Western Darfur and Chad, speaking their own Nilo-Saharan language. In the nineteenth century, after the fall of the Fur sultanate, they established their own sultanate, and still have their own sultan. Many Masalit migrated eastwards during and after the colonial era.
Masalat/ Masalati	Masalit group living in the Gereida area of Southern Darfur, under a different traditional leader from that of the western Masalit

Mbororo

Nomadic Fulbe-speaking pastoralists widely dispersed in Sudan and in countries to the west. Some Sudanese Mbororo have links to Tulus in South Darfur and in the dry season they traverse the whole of Raga county at its western extremity, going as far south as Equatoria.

Misseriya Jebel

Smaller group with origin stories in Jebel Mun, on the western border of North Darfur. They speak a Nilo-Saharan language related to Tama, and say that they are linked to both Tama and Misseriya groups—the latter one of the biggest Arabic-speaking cattle-keeping groups in Sudan. Some moved south in the droughts of the 1970s and 1980s. Some live in eastern Jebel Marra.

nazir

Paramount chief, the highest rank in the northern of Native Administration, the system of rule through traditional authorities established under British rule.

NCP

National Congress Party, created by the Ingaz regime in 1997 and the ruling party in Khartoum since that time.

Niger-Congo languages

Language family that includes most sub-Saharan languages.

Nilotic

Group of languages and cultures of East Africa. The group includes Nuer, Dinka, Shilluk and Acholi, who probably comprise a majority of the population of Southern Sudan, but do not constitute a distinct political community.

Nilo-Saharan languages

Family of languages spoken mainly in Sudan and Sahelian countries.

Njagulgule, Ngulinguli

Smaller ethnic group with origin stories linked to Darfur. Their language is the same as the Beigo language of Darfur and they have a Beigo leading family: they may have been Beigo clients. They lived in Jebel Liri, east of the Kafia Kingi enclave, but moved south to the Raga area. In 1987 most of them were displaced to Raga town.

omda

See *umda*.

PCA

Permanent Court of Arbitration, The Hague.

PDF

Popular Defence Forces. In the 1980s, these local militias were formed from tribal elements in northern Sudan to fight the war in the south. Under the current government, they became a legally recognized force that included urban militia formations linked to the regime.

Raga — Capital of Raga county.

Raga county — One of four counties in Western Bahr al-Ghazal state; includes the Kafia Kingi enclave. (See note on the area under study.)

Rizeigat/ Rizayqat — One of the Arabic-speaking cattle-keeping groups (Baggara) in Darfur and Chad. The Rizeigat area covers most of south-eastern Darfur. Origin narratives in Arabia or Tunisia; they arrived in Sudan in the seventeenth or eighteenth century and once constituted one of the biggest political communities in South Darfur. They share their name with a related camel-keeping group of North Darfur.

SAF — Sudan Armed Forces, the main legally-recognized army of the Khartoum government.

SANU — Sudan African National Union, Southern Sudanese political party with a generally separatist agenda, founded in the 1960s.

SDP — Sudanese Old Pound, currency in northern Sudan until 1992 and in Southern Sudan until 2007; replaced in both regions in January 2007 by the new Sudanese Pound (SDG), in accordance with the CPA.

SLA — Sudan Liberation Army, a Darfur rebel group that split into many factions, some of which signed the DPA with the government in 2006.

shaykh — Third tier chief in northern system of Native Administration; in Arabic and Islamic countries, the word may refer to an elder, notable or religious leader.

SPLA — Sudan People's Liberation Army, military wing of the rebel SPLM that became a legally-recognized army under the terms of the CPA.

SPLM — Sudan People's Liberation Movement, rebelled against the Government of Sudan in Southern Sudan in 1983 and entered government after signing the CPA in 2005.

SSU — Sudan Socialist Union, party founded in 1972 as the basis of a single-party regime that lasted until 1985.

sultan	Title for a chief in Southern Native Administration in some areas of the south; also title for rulers of Sahelian states of the seventeenth to twentieth centuries. In this paper, Southern sultans are where possible called chiefs.
Taysha	Baggara (Arabic-speaking cattle-keeping) group in the far west of South Darfur. Origin narratives in Tunisia or Arabia; played an important role in the Mahdiya; links with Kara people.
takhzin	System whereby merchants stockpile commodities during the wet season, when transport of goods is most difficult and prices are consequently high.
Tama	Smaller group living in north-west Darfur and mostly in Chad. They speak a Nilo-Saharan language, Tama, and are linguistically linked to the Erenga and Misseriya Jebel groups. Some moved to South Darfur as a result of the droughts of the 1970s and 1980s.
Turkiya	Arabic name for the Turco-Egyptian regime, 1820–1882.
umda	Omda, second-tier chief in the northern system of Native Administration.
umudiya	Omodiya, a second-tier chiefship.
UNESCO	United Nations Educational, Scientific and Cultural Organization.
Western Bahr al-Ghazal	One of the ten southern states. (See note on the area under study.)
Western district	Western district of Bahr al-Ghazal state. (See note on the area under study.)
WSP	Western Savannah Project, a development project in South Darfur in the 1970s and 1980s.
Wadai	Sultanate founded in the sixteenth century, in what is now Chad.
Yulu	Smaller tribe, with origin story linking it to locations in present-day CAR; moved from Kafia Kingi to Deim Jallab in 1930; displaced in 1960s but resettled in Kafia Kingi in 2002. Language closely related to Binga and Kara.

Zaghawa	Larger ethnic group, speaking a Nilo-Saharan language. Since the sixteenth century, they have lived in semi-arid areas of North Darfur and Chad; associated with camel and sheep pastoralism. Drought displaced some of them to the northern edge of the Kafia Kingi enclave in the 1970s, from where many were displaced in 2006 during the civil war in Darfur.
Zande	Large ethnolinguistic group in south-western Sudan, northern DRC and eastern CAR. Zande states were established in the eighteenth and nineteenth century, led by an elite with origins to the east who incorporated indigenous ethnic groups.
zariba	Enclosure fenced with thorns; slaving fort during the era of the Turkiya.

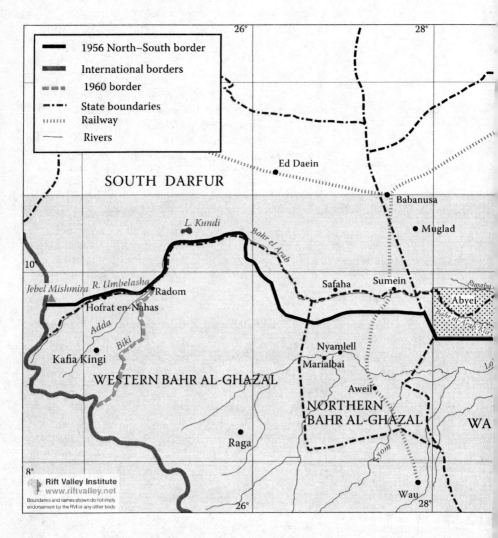

Map 3. *Sudan: North–South border with area of detailed map*